Magic Moments

Stories, Lessons & Memories from a Twenty-Year Career at Walt Disney World

Michael Lyons

Theme Park Press
The Happiest Books on Earth
www.ThemeParkPress.com

© 2023 Michael Lyons

No part of this publication may be reproduced, distributed, or transmitted in any form or by any means, including photocopying, recording, or other electronic or mechanical methods, without the prior written permission of the publisher, except for brief quotations embodied in critical reviews and certain other non-commercial uses permitted by copyright law.

Although every precaution has been taken to verify the accuracy of the information contained herein, no responsibility is assumed for any errors or omissions, and no liability is assumed for damages that may result from the use of this information.

Theme Park Press is not associated with the Walt Disney Company.

The views expressed in this book are those of the author and do not necessarily reflect the views of Theme Park Press.

Theme Park Press publishes its books in a variety of print and electronic formats. Some content that appears in one format may not appear in another.

Editor: Bob McLain
Layout: Artisanal Text

ISBN 978-1-68390-338-3
Printed in the United States of America

Theme Park Press | www.ThemeParkPress.com
Address queries to bob@themeparkpress.com

*For my Mom, Kay Lyons,
and my Dad and Stepmom, Bill and Sandy Lyons.
Thank you for your love and for
letting me follow my Disney dreams.*

Contents

Introduction vii

1. "You're as Welcome as Can Be" 1
2. "Once Upon a Time…Is Now!" 11
3. "Four" Score 23
4. "Y'All Come Back, Ya Hear?!" 43
5. "With Great Power Comes Great Responsibility" 59
6. More Than a Numbers Game 73
7. Jiminy and Obi-Wan Were Right 87
8. "We Have to Watch Out for Each Other" 95
9. The Combined Effort 103
10. Storm Season 117
11. The Light Is Still Burning 137
12. "If We Weren't So Down, We'd Up and Leave" 149
13. "Every Bit of Life Is Lit by Fortuosity" 161
14. "Keep Moving Forward" 171

Bibliography 175
Acknowledgments 179
About the Author 181

Introduction
"Simply Mad About the Mouse"

"We're here!" My dad excitedly said that to me as we entered the Magic Kingdom on our first Walt Disney World trip.

It was 1987, and after a little over two decades of being a "Disney kid" who went to see all of the studio's films, watched all of their shows, wore a lot of their T-shirts, and bought as much of their merchandise as I could find, I was, at the ripe young age of 21 walking under the train station and on to Main Street, U.S.A. My very first glimpse at the Magic Kingdom in person.

"We're here!" said my dad with no attempt to hide any enthusiasm. It perfectly summed up how my dad (another confessed Disney fan), and I felt at that moment.

I had not thought at all, at that time, that thirteen years later, I would be *working* on that magical street.

That vacation in 1987, the first time I had ever been on a plane and the farthest I had ever traveled from my home in Long Island, NY, was an awakening for me in many ways. After returning home, I began to think of Disney not only as something that meant so much to me as a fan but also as a place where I could and would like to work someday.

Flash-forward to the fall of 2000. I drove from New York to Orlando in two days, with almost everything I owned crammed into my Chevy Cavalier (yes, I was really into those sexy sports cars that could go 0 to 60 in thirty minutes). I tried to see out of my back window, but my Gateway computer, sitting on top of boxes and covered in a blanket, was blocking my way. What was ahead of me, however, was clear.

I was going to work at the Walt Disney World Resort.

Despite the traffic in the Washington, D.C. area, there was no stopping me, and that was my goal.

My earliest memory of falling in love with the magic of Disney was during that most magical time of the year as a kid—summer vacations from school.

It all started with "The Walt Disney Summer Film Festival." Don't worry, you didn't miss some traditional, critic-led festival on the shores of Cannes, France. This series of Disney double features came around to local movie theaters for five summers in the 1970s.

But apparently, it only happened in the New York area, as the Disney Studio had difficulty distributing their films in New York. To remedy this and increase the audience for their films in this area, Disney partnered with local movie theaters, who agreed to host the "Summer Film Festival" from late June through Labor Day. Each week would feature a different Disney double feature, one animated film, and one live action.[1]

Thanks to this, I could "binge" almost every Disney film, back when binging meant that your parents took you to the Mayfair Movie Theater in Commack, NY, where every other kid in the neighborhood was gathered shoulder to shoulder in a crowded theater.

Over those five years, thanks to my supportive parents, I was able to see such memorable double features as *Cinderella* with *Mary Poppins* and *The Jungle Book* with *Swiss Family Robinson*, and such eclectic pair-ups as *Snow White and the Seven Dwarfs* with *Blackbeard's Ghost* and *Robin Hood* with *That Darn Cat*.

Seeing these films on the big screen showed me a world that ignited my imagination. Between trips to the theater, there was *The Wonderful World of Disney* on Sunday nights, Disney stuffed animals, board games, mouse ears, and record albums.

One of the latter was *Mickey Mouse: This is Your Life*, which my dad bought for me. It was a Disneyland Storyteller book and record set, which told of Mickey's career, and this nattily dressed man who had something to do with the Mouse's success.

Walt Disney.

---

[1] Jerry Beck, "Disney 1970s Summer Film Festivals," *Cartoon Brew*, cartoonbrew.com, October 1, 2008, (accessed May 12, 2023).

When I realized a man was responsible for all of this, I began to want to learn more about him, especially after finding *The Disney Films* by Leonard Maltin at a Scholastic Book Fair (there was magic at those, too!).

As I read and devoured more about Walt and this Kingdom he created, I began to set my sights on someday working for Disney. My goal was to be a Disney animator eventually. One thing was holding me back: any inkling of talent, one *needs* to *be* an animator.

As I got older, my interest in Disney only increased through the treacherous years of junior high and formative years of high school. However, in the late 70s and early 80s, being a teenager and being a Disney fan didn't go hand-in-hand.

If word had gotten out about this, I probably would have been thrown into my locker more times than I already was. Today, Disney transcends generations, and it's acceptable and cool to be a fan at any age. That wasn't the case then, so my Disney fandom was something I held close to the vest.

As I went to college, at first latching on to that most eventually unlucrative of majors—"undecided," I ultimately transitioned to an English literature major and a business minor, which I guess was preparing me to someday manage a store that sold the complete works of William Shakespeare.

I was somewhat directionless and rudderless. Any thought or daydream I had to become a Disney animator faded away with my high school art classes, and I just kept hoping that college would last for a while, or I would be bequeathed a dream job.

Then came that Walt Disney World vacation in 1987. Not only did it slake a lifelong thirst for Disney, but while I was there, I couldn't help but notice that people were working there, lots and lots of people working there.

Hey, I thought as my career canoe seemed to be taking on water, *Maybe I could work here, too?*

When I returned home to New York, I felt I finally had a direction. I began researching what it took to work at Walt Disney World and did the late 80s version of searching safari on my phone – I went to the library.

I went through articles in the microfiche machine, like an FBI agent solving a crime, and I knew that the day after graduation, I would be packing up everything in my car and driving to Orlando, FL.

Around this time, I bought a cassette tape (which was kind of like a tangible, plastic version of iTunes) called *Simply Mad About the Mouse*. On it were versions of classic Disney songs like "When You Wish Upon a Star," sung by Billy Joel, "Someday My Prince Will Come" by En Vogue, and "Who's Afraid of the Big Bad Wolf" by LL Cool J.

If this sounds like an incredible '90s mashup "of-its-time" nostalgia, it is. But I listened to it in my car non-stop, and it became the soundtrack of my time focused on working for Disney.

These visits to the library also helped me unearth books and articles, allowing me to learn more about the rich history of the Disney company and Walt Disney himself.

But, while all of this was going on, something else happened. One of my professors, Sister Loretta, at St. Joseph's College, returning one of the papers I had turned in for class, said, "You write well. You should consider writing for the school newspaper."

I gave it a shot, writing reviews of shows, singers and comedians who would appear at school. This led to me reviewing movies for a local newspaper, *The Island Ear*, which was complimentary in movie theaters (and usually left on the theater seats after every show).

From here, I pitched article ideas to other movie magazines, and soon, I was working as a freelance writer. But, going down this road meant that I had veered off the "Disney Career Turnpike."

However, I still loved Disney and sought any opportunity to write about it. In the winter of 1994, an editor of one of the magazines I wrote for called me and said, "Hey, you know Disney. They have a movie called *The Lion King* coming out this summer. Would you like to cover it for us?"

I wanted to answer, "Yeah, I know. I have been watching the trailer on the *Pinocchio* VHS non-stop! Um, yeah, I will cover it!"

And so, "it all started with *The Lion King*." For the next seven years, I covered each new Disney and, eventually, Pixar animated feature that was released. I had the incredible opportunity to interview the Studio's animators, directors, producers, art directors, and executives (including Roy E. Disney!). They had all been heroes and inspirations to me and having the opportunity to spend quality time with them, capture their insights and share them with others is an experience I will never forget.

Additionally, I had the good fortune to write about other movies and television shows, interviewing many talented artists working in the industry.

It was an incredible time. I was riding high, by-line after by-line. Then, something happened.

The World Wide Web.

Remember that? Remember when it first became "a thing?"

That good ol' "Information Superhighway" (there's another flashback!).

As the internet became a part of our everyday lives, more and more of the magazines I wrote for transitioned to putting more of their content on their websites. As they did, there wasn't as much of a need for freelance writers.

And so, the writing assignments started to disappear slowly. But, my love of Disney did not, and my mind shifted back to relocating to Florida and working for Walt Disney World (plus some of the winters in the late '90s were beginning to look like scenes out of National Geographic documentaries about Antarctica. I needed some warm weather).

I started applying for Walt Disney World jobs that seemed even remotely connected to writing. I even began mailing my resume to different departments with a cover letter expressing my interest.

I was getting nowhere.

I began to see light at the end of the tunnel for a Disney job during a Walt Disney World visit for a writing assignment. I was covering an event celebrating the 85th birthday of Disney Legend Marc Davis, one of Walt's top animators, who had worked on such classic films as *Snow White and the Seven Dwarfs*, *Peter Pan*, and *101 Dalmatians*. Additionally, Marc was one of the first theme park Imagineers who helped to create such attractions as Pirates of the Caribbean and The Haunted Mansion.

I was so lucky to interview Marc and wound up talking with his Disney Tour Guide, a Guest Relations Cast Member, who assists the visiting V.I.P. His name was Dana, and I spoke with him about how much I wanted to work for Disney.

Dana told me, "You should consider moving down here and getting a job as a Cast Member in one of the parks or resorts. Disney loves to hire from within."

And that thought rolled around inside my mind the entire weekend I was at Walt Disney World, the whole flight home, and for weeks afterward.

But could I do that? Leave my family and friends behind, change gears from writing to something completely different? Just pack my stuff, get in my car, and move to Florida?

Six months later, as I made the twenty-four-hour drive over two days, with my mom, navigating and keeping me caffeinated, I found out that the answer was…Yes.

What follows in this book is what happened during my Walt Disney World career over the next twenty years. As the subtitle states, my goal with this book is to provide "Stories, Lessons, and Memories."

This book is a combination of my love of writing and storytelling with my love for working with Disney. Additionally, whenever I tell someone I worked for Disney, they usually respond with, "Oh! What was that like?" Here's the answer in the pages that follow.

The Disney Parks and Resorts do so much so well that people, especially fans and frequent visitors, want to know *how* they do it. I wanted to include that here in this book. However, my goal is not to give away *everything* but to share methodologies behind how Disney gets things done.

Additionally, and maybe even more importantly, I don't want to pull back the curtain to the point that Walt Disney World magic is diminished. If you are looking for the "real story," a "tell all," or "secrets revealed," don't look here. This is all about the specialness of a highly unique destination. It is never my intention to lessen the Walt Disney World experience for anyone.

The Walt Disney World resort, like all areas of the company, fulfills Walt's wish to always be evolving, and because of this, some of what I discuss may no longer be in effect. Here, however, I am discussing what was in place during my time with Disney, from 2000 through 2020.

There is also official nomenclature when it comes to Disney (such as the fact that the Magic Kingdom is officially Magic Kingdom Park, and the entire property is the Walt Disney World Resort). As another of my goals is to keep the tone of this book very conversational, I don't always rely on official names of parks, resorts and other areas of Walt Disney World.

In my two decades with the company, I learned something each day, which is why I wanted to share lessons. Through successful and not-so-successful moments, there was always something that I took away from the experience that helped me in the future and that I could share with others, as well.

Was every day perfect while working at Walt Disney World? To answer that, I ask, "Is every day perfect at *your* job?"

Like anywhere else, there were disagreements, frustrations, stressful moments, personality clashes, and all the other unfortunate baggage that gets packed in the luggage at so many other workplaces.

These moments' challenging details have been left out of this book and remain only in my memory. Would you *want* to read a book that focused on or included those?

Instead, here, I look at some challenges I faced, the positive outcome that resulted, what I learned, and what I hope you can learn by sharing them in the following chapters.

There's no focus here *at all* on the negative. If you are looking for that, there are plenty of other places to find it.

Speaking of positive, that brings me to the memories.

So many people positively impacted my life during my years at Disney, and many of them have become dear friends. Being fortunate enough to work at all four Walt Disney World theme parks, Disney Springs, and even off-site locations like the Disney shops at Orlando International Airport allowed me to be lucky enough to craft unforgettable memories.

They may be overtly upbeat and filtered through extremely rose-colored glasses as I discuss them. Some may even find them extremely *Pollyana* (the first of many subtle and not-so-subtle Disney references in these pages, feel free to score yourself a point for each one).

The cynics may roll their eyes into the backs of their head, as I do indeed take a positive perspective when discussing my memories of working at Disney. Honestly, that's how I remember all of it.

While the book does begin with my first Walt Disney World work days, it isn't set up chronologically. Instead, each chapter has a topic, and I share related stories and memories and conclude with lessons to pass on.

So now, please keep all hands and arms inside the book as we embark on *Magic Moments: Stories, Lessons & Memories from a Twenty-Year Career at Walt Disney World*.

Or, in the immortal words of my dad: "We're here!"

CHAPTER ONE

"You're as Welcome as Can Be"
First Day at Disney

It's the first day of school. Anxiety is high. The unknown is unnerving. You're scared.

Remember those feelings? From kindergarten through college, they would re-surface with the end of every summer vacation. As adults, those feelings return to us each time we start a new job and walk into that first day of work. Oh sure, the thought of having the teacher everyone dreads, learning that algebra you've avoided (and will never again use), and your tuna sandwich sweating its way through your paper lunch bag may not be significant factors anymore. However, those first-day *feelings* are still there.

Just *finding* your way to a new job can be daunting. Then, locating the parking lot, your workplace, the nearest restroom, the cafeteria, and not knowing a soul—all of these things that will soon be rote, seem as strange as visiting a different country.

But, you have filled out the application, submitted the resume, and aced the interview. Now, you have the job.

And…it's the first day of school…all over again. The anxiety, the unknown, the not knowing…*anything.*

Wouldn't it be nice if the first day of work brought your anxiety *down*, gave you the information you need without being overwhelming, and made everything a lot less scary? On top of that, imagine if you were made to feel a *part* of something, and that something meant so much to so many (including you) and that you felt not just part of a company, but as overused as it may seem, part of a family (insert your eye roll here, if you'd like, but it's a thing).

That was the first day of work at the Walt Disney World Resort.

Unlike many other jobs, in which you may report right to the workplace and receive a brief overview ("Here are the keys, lock up when you're done!"), on your first day of work at Walt Disney World, you report to a classroom.

"Disney Traditions" is the name of the class that *all* new employees, called Cast Members, attend on their first day of work at the Walt Disney World Resort. It doesn't matter *what* you will be doing in your new job—operating an attraction, performing in a show, sweeping a street, or ringing sales at a cash register in a shop—or *where* you will be working—in one of the four theme parks, as a secretary, in the finance department, with marketing, as a manager, or an executive—you don't go to your work location on that first day.

You go to Disney University.

Don't worry, you didn't miss a school, even a "safety school," when applying to colleges. This may sound like an accredited institution, but it's something different and fundamental to the experience for all new Disney Cast Members.

This building is located "behind the scenes" or "backstage" at Walt Disney World. Like the word university in its namesake, Disney University is filled with classrooms, each used for some form of instructor-led training that will assist new Cast Members in their new role.

Disney University is bursting with the rich history of The Disney Company, as framed photographs of Walt Disney, his brother Roy and all their many accomplishments, from iconic characters through the early Walt Disney World opening day pictures, are framed on the wall.

As you make your way to Traditions class, these are like coming attractions posters of what you are about to experience.

The goal of Disney Traditions is to, quite literally, set the stage and make sure that all Cast Members start their Walt Disney World work experience the same way. This eight-hour class builds the foundation for all that's to come.

The all-day session takes its first day Cast Members through the philosophy, the values, the verbiage, and the history behind the new role they are about to step into. It also provides information on what to expect when they arrive at their work location, or better yet, what visitors, or "Guests," as they are called, can expect from them when they come to Disney.

When a new Cast Member walks out of Traditions class at the end of that first day, they not only have more information than they had when they walked into the classroom that morning, they're not only ready for their first day "on the job," but, in every way, they *know* they're working for Disney. You just *feel* it as you leave the class.

Traditions isn't just an instructor with a pointer walking everyone through a monotone "spiel" while gesturing to a PowerPoint. The class, like Walt Disney World itself, has energy.

Just as the lyric from the "Mickey Mouse Club March" stated: "You're as welcome as can be…" and that welcoming spirit fills the classroom.

I still recall my Traditions class vividly. One of those memories that never fades. It's your first day working for Disney, and it's a date that, for all Cast Members, remains as instantly easy to recall as their birthday.

Mine was October 3, 2000, and, instead of someone appearing at the front of the room and announcing, "Good Morning," the lights dimmed as the classroom filled with equally unsure first day Cast Members quickly hushed. A video with fast-paced images of every corner of Walt Disney World appeared on the screen.

After ending in a crescendo, a gentleman in a suit and tie walked to the front of the classroom and announced, as if we were all about to board the latest Disney attraction (which, in many ways, we were): "Good morning! Welcome to Traditions!"

I still remember him to this day; his name was Brian, he worked in entertainment and a nervous, "first day-er" couldn't have asked for a more perfect embodiment of what a Cast Member could be.

Brian seemed like all the open, welcoming, and friendly Cast Members I had encountered as a Guest during my many Walt Disney World visits. He *would* be all those during Traditions, and he would also be informative and encouraging.

One of the main facets that Brian would discuss during the morning portion of Traditions was how working for Disney was so different than working…well…anywhere else.

This has been a differentiator for Disney Parks around the globe since Walt Disney opened Disneyland on July 17, 1955.

Walt discussed how the idea for Disneyland started with his biographer, Bob Thomas:

"'It all started when my daughters were very young, and I took them to amusement parks on Sunday. I sat on a bench eating peanuts and looking around me. I said to myself, dammit, why can't there be a better place to take your children, where you can have fun together?'"[1]

And so, Walt did research, visiting amusement parks, zoos, and fairs. Still, he was often disappointed, as not only wasn't the family able to enjoy the experience together, but many times, the experience wasn't very good. Upkeep and maintenance were often lacking, trash would litter the ground, and surly was the best way to describe the staff.

Then, Walt visited Tivoli Gardens in Copenhagen with his wife, Lillian. As Thomas writes, this was a turning point: "The gaiety of the music, the excellence of the food and drink, the warm courtesy of the employees—everything combined for a pleasurable experience. 'Now, this is what an amusement place should be!' Walt enthused to Lilly."[2]

These early thoughts from Walt about what would make Disneyland unique would allow the name Disney to become synonymous with excellence in so many regards: service, standards, cleanliness, and experience for almost seventy years.

Walt wanted Disneyland to be entertainment, for all, no different than his television show or his films. Gone would be the days when visitors would be treated poorly and how that would be a stigma of coming to an amusement park. Now these visitors would be treated like Guests coming over to your home. Apologies would be given for inconveniences, and those inconveniences would be rectified.

Guests wouldn't just walk into a haphazard cluster of Ferris wheels and roller coasters. Walt challenged his artists (dubbed "Imagineers," combining the words "imagination" and

---

[1] Bob Thomas, *Walt Disney: An American Original* (New York, Hyperion, 1994), p.11.
[2] Ibid, p.241.

"engineering") who designed the park to take everything they had done on Disney *film* and bring it to life on Disney *land*.

Each area of the park would look like a movie set, and there would even be background music playing, as there would be in a movie. There would be a theme for each area—Main Street, U.S.A. would reflect America at the turn-of-the-last century, Frontierland, the old west, Fantasyland, fairy tales, and fables, etc.

This wasn't an *amusement* park; it was a *theme* park.

And all this culture would carry seamlessly over to Walt Disney World when it opened on October 1, 1971, almost five years after Walt Disney's death.

So, as a Cast Member, how do they carry on and support this legacy of all that a visit to Walt Disney World stands for and means for so many? That's what the first portion of Traditions was about to teach us.

The class began with what would be unique about working for Disney. As we were working for an entertainment company, we learned immediately that we were referred to as Cast Members, not employees. We weren't hired, we were *cast* in a role in the show that is Walt Disney World. This title of Cast Member would soon make sense, as did the other jargon that would quickly become part of our everyday vernacular.

We wouldn't be wearing "uniforms"; we would have "costumes"; we wouldn't be working "out in the area" or "on the floor," we would be working "on stage"; offices, stockrooms, kitchens, and the like wouldn't be "behind the scenes," they would be "backstage."

Like Disney's films, characters, and television shows, the theme parks are part of that world of entertainment, and, as Cast Members, we were a part of it, too. And everything we did, including the verbiage we used reflected that.

Just like going to Walt Disney World as a Guest for the first time is distinctive compared to visiting another amusement park, so is working at Walt Disney World as compared to working elsewhere, and Traditions serves as a bridge into this workplace.

From here, we all received an infectious "crash course" in Disney history. If you aren't fluent or familiar with Disney history before Traditions, you will leave with a cursory knowledge, and maybe even more.

Because there is a lot here: we were taken from Walt Disney's birth on December 5, 1901, to the creation of Mickey Mouse in 1928, *Snow White and the Seven Dwarfs* in 1937, Walt embarking on a television show in 1954, the opening of Disneyland in 1955, Walt's death in 1966, Walt Disney World's opening on October 1, 1971, the subsequent parks after (including those internationally), and the launch of the Disney Cruise Line (which was, then, one of the newest additions at the end of the timeline).

And those are just some of the few points of Disney history that were covered. After watching our facilitator "walk" us through (then) almost a hundred years of Disney history and watching a video compilation filled with every corner of the company, it was hard not to feel a sense of being a part of something and wanting to know more.

More is what we were about to learn. As fascinating as the history of Disney is, for those of us about to work at the Resort and interact with Guests daily, chances were good that they weren't going to approach us one day and ask, "Excuse me, sir. I have a problem. I desperately need to know when Tokyo Disneyland opened!" (April 15, 1983, just to save you a trip to Wikipedia).

Those fun trivia questions might surface, but most likely, Guests would have more practical questions and concerns. How could we assist them while being part of this rich company history and themed story that was Walt Disney World, of which we were now a part?

We would assist those Guests with keys, four of them, to be exact.

There is so much to consider each day as a Walt Disney World Cast Member, and Traditions provides all new to the company with a way to categorize these considerations:

▷ Safety
▷ Courtesy
▷ Show
▷ Efficiency

Disney termed these "The Four Keys" to a great Cast and Guest experience and to set up *all* Cast for success. These Keys could easily be used as a filter and prioritize all Cast Members' responsibilities.

These Four Keys become the guidepost, and delving into them in Traditions serves as a first introduction to working as a Cast Member.

In Traditions, we also discussed Respect Appreciate and Value Everyone (R.A.V.E.), and this has been an essential part of the company culture. Working at Walt Disney World with peers from not only different parts of the country but of the world, is genuinely an edification for every Cast Member, every day. In 2020, there was the introduction of a fifth key, Inclusion. Disney has always been focused on the diversity of their Guests and their Cast, and this Key made perfect sense as an addition. While still a part of our everyday workplace, Inclusion was not one of the Keys during my tenure at Disney, and the next chapter will focus on the Four Keys that were in place while I was with Disney.

As the Traditions afternoon began to wind down, there was almost a sense of graduating that began to sink in. Cast Members are presented with something akin to turning the tassel on their graduation cap. This "something" was our nametag. Before nametags were passed out, everyone in the room who had been excited previously at the mere possibilities of working at Walt Disney World was now eyeing Brian's nametag, wondering what ours would look like.

Many of us had been to Walt Disney World as Guests, and we knew the importance of that nametag. When a Guest spotted a nametag, they could get directions and ask questions. Cast Members knew that when they put that nametag on, especially for that first time and all time, they were a part of Disney.

Brian handed out the nametags like diplomas. And there was mine, just as I had seen so many times on others while I was on vacation. Was a shaft of light cast across it as a heavenly choir sang "When You Wish Upon a Star" playing in the background? In my mind, yes.

"MICHAEL"
"Port Jefferson Station, N.Y."

There it was, my name and hometown, right below the "Walt Disney World 2000" logo up top, that was in place for the Millennium celebration (remember that Disney fans? Where we would "Celebrate the Future Hand-in-Hand?"). And with that, Traditions neared its end. But there wouldn't be a bell that would ring, followed by a "class dismissed" declaration. Instead, Brian shared some closing thoughts and told a personal story about his most impactful moment as a Cast Member. Then, the lights dimmed again, and another video appeared on the screen.

This one played slower, evocative music, accompanied by gentler images of Guests enjoying Walt Disney World and making memories. It faded to black, and lights came back on, like the conclusion of a Disney movie, leaving one with that same hopeful, positive feeling.

As Brian congratulated us all on being Cast Members, we all applauded. And with that applause, we signaled the end of our first day's journey, as we were then met by Cast Members named Coordinators of Training, who served as our guides for the next part of our training.

These were Cast Members from different areas throughout Walt Disney World who had the critical job of, just as their title stated, coordinating all aspects of a new Cast Member's training. These Coordinators of Training would meet with Cast coming to their location to discuss the next steps.

As rote as it may sound, Traditions taught me a lesson in how important first impressions are and how important that first day at a new job can be. The expression, "You don't get a second chance to make a first impression," is well-worn because we really don't.

Of course, like the end of any first day at any job, there was still the unknown, but now there was much less of it. As newly "ordained" Cast Members, who had just met in class, a group of us stood outside in the parking lot of Disney University, talking about the day and where we would be working.

We attempted to straighten our new nametags and make them look more like those of the veterans who made their way to their cars on, what was for them, another Tuesday. We eventually said our goodbyes and walked to our cars and our own different Disney journeys.

Traditions was a perfect "dipping of your toe" into the Walt Disney World pool, and you couldn't help but have the sense one usually has after their first day of work. "OK, now what?"

The answer was the education that was to follow, including an appreciation for the value of teaching and the kindness of others.

CHAPTER TWO

"Once Upon a Time...Is Now!"
On-the-Job Training at Disney

A schedule!

There it was, not just *a* schedule, *my* schedule! Traditions felt like graduation; my nametag was akin to my diploma, and now I was working for Walt Disney World, and I had received...

A schedule!

After the conclusion of Traditions class, we all received a schedule detailing the rest of our training. *A schedule!* We knew exactly what we would do and, more importantly, *where* we would go.

For me, that was a return to Disney University and another class. Nope, I wouldn't be heading to my work location just yet. I was going to be working in Merchandise at one of the shops at Walt Disney World. But, before going to my location, I was going to "Merchantainment." This was a then all-day class that prepared all new Merchandise Cast Members on the basics *before* going to their area.

I truly felt like a real "insider," figuring out that the class title was merging the words Merchandise with the entertainment that Disney is known for. Then, the next day, I was deflated when the question "What does Merchantainment stand for?" was asked, and everyone responded before I had the chance to show off my epiphany from the day before.

While the class title may not surprise many, the class itself was another ingenious training example of setting up new Cast Members for success. The classroom was divided between a standard classroom setting and a recreation of a merchandise shop, complete with rows of cash registers and shelves stocked with merchandise.

Throughout the day, we were again versed in Disney's philosophies and learned how to apply them while performing the technical aspects of our job. It's important to note that at this point in my life, I was someone who was not well-versed in retail.

In fact, it had been about seventeen years since I worked near a cash register or assisted a customer. Of course, I was great at *being* a shopper, but the thought of *helping* a Guest who was going to be one, in a Walt Disney World shop, where we would be...like...around people...well, the characters of Pain and Panic from *Hercules* were doing laps in my mind.

That's what made Merchantainment such a relief. In the classroom, I was with a knowledgeable facilitator named Penny and other new Merchandise Cast Members who were also hangin' with Pain and Panic.

Penny joked about what it was like to have a name like that while working in Merchandise. Like Brian from my Traditions class, Penny was a great role model, someone we aspired to be like. Also, like Brian, she worked another role at Walt Disney World, and wouldn't you know it, she worked in Merchandise. She taught the class on a "cross-utilization basis" when not working her full-time job in one of the Merchandise shops at the resort. As she took us through the day, she shared stories from her own experiences, not only adding a sense of credibility but also setting what we were doing throughout the day against a "real world" backdrop ("Wow! Someone can process a traveler's check and live to tell about it?!")

Throughout the day, we were able to "role play," with one of us playing a Cast Member and one of us playing Guest, processing mock transactions. By the end of the day, it all didn't seem as palpitation-inducing as it did when we walked through the door.

Some may say "C'mon!" when they hear that using a register scanner or figuring out how a Guest pays with a credit card can be daunting, but we have all done something for the first time. And doing that in the "safe space" of a classroom makes it all better.

We learned what the SKU number of an item (near the bar code), stands for. It's Stock Keeping Unit (throw that around at the next cocktail party). We learned the best way to give a Guest change or how to "Count Change The Disney Way" (you count up from the amount of the sale to the bill the Guest gave you, and you can't go wrong). And, it was so long ago, that we also learned how to process a check payment (that was once like a paper version of Apple Pay).

While doing all this, we also learned how to balance Courtesy with the technical part of our role. At the start of the day, we were focused on something so seemingly simple as making sure the receipt printed. As the day ended, we were watching the receipt print and asking our "pretend Guest" standing in front of us, "How has your day been?" *at the same time* and feeling so great about ourselves for this amazing feat of multitasking.

It felt good to leave the Merchantainment class with less Pain and Panic and more "I Can Go the Distance" reverberating in my mind. According to my schedule, I was heading to my work location the following day. Yup, bright and early, just about fifteen hours later, I'd be at…

The Magic Kingdom.

I had been hired as a Merchandise Host on Main Street, U.S.A. Just about a week prior, I applied for the job at the "Casting Center" (again, keeping in the theme, Walt Disney World isn't hiring you as a prospective employee, you are being "Cast in a role, in the show").

The Walt Disney World recruiter asked me if I preferred a specific work location. I gave a lot of thought, weighing several different options, even applying a scientific method, and provided a brilliant answer, "Well…I enjoy shopping…in the shops at Walt Disney World…"

"Great," she replied, typing on her keyboard, and looking on her computer screen to inform me at there was an opening in Magic Kingdom Merchandise on Main Street, U.S.A.

"Great," I replied as calmly as I could. Meanwhile, in my mind was a vision of me, standing in the middle of Main Street U.S.A., spinning in a circle, with my arms extended, while fireworks exploded in the sky around Cinderella Castle behind me.

Main Street, U.S.A.?! The Magic Kingdom?! My favorite land in my favorite Disney Park. I loved how Main Street, U.S.A. served as the gateway to all else that the Magic Kingdom held and how it was such a close connection to Walt Disney himself, as it reflected his hometown of Marceline, MO, where he grew up.

As the performers sing in the land itself, I'd be "...walkin' right down the middle of Main Street, U.S.A."

The recruiter informed me that she had other options. "Nope," I replied—this was perfect.

And now, I was back at Disney University for my third day of work, an orientation class dubbed "Once Upon a Time... is Now," which would introduce a group of other new Cast Members and me to the Magic Kingdom. We were all working in different lines of business and roles, but we all had something in common, we were all working at the Magic Kingdom.

The goal of the class was to, once again, ground us in the entertainment and theming that was such a large part of our role, by providing the story (and details) behind the Magic Kingdom, that Walt had first introduced with Disneyland and which his team of Imagineers had carried on after Walt.

We were also going to learn a crucial part of our new jobs: how to get around "backstage" at the Magic Kingdom. After all, it's so much easier to deliver on Walt Disney's dream when you know where you are going.

Our host for "Once Upon a Time" was a gentleman named Randy, who brought with him a sense of Disney magic that seemed innate along with energy and humor that was infectious. There was no one better to take us on a grand circle tour of this most Magical of Kingdoms.

We all boarded a bus and started our tour at the mythical tunnel (dubbed the "Utilidor") that runs underneath the Magic Kingdom. When Walt Disney World was built, planning included allowing Cast Members to get around quickly and efficiently throughout the park without disrupting the Show. Additionally, there was a need to house much of the park's infrastructure, including pipes, electric cables, a trash disposal system, and computer systems that control the innumerable Audio-Animatronic figures in the attractions. [3]

---

[3] Jeff Kurtti, *Since the World Began: Walt Disney World The First 25 Years*, (New York, Hyperion, 1996). P. 26.

With the water tables in Florida so high, the Utilidor had to be built on top of the ground, so the Magic Kingdom was built on top of this, basically placing it on the second floor.[4]

Many Walt Disney World Guests and Disney fans in general wonder about those "tunnels" that run underneath. Are they among the many "Disney myths?"

I am here as a "myth buster!" That's too grand a term, or I am a "myth debunker," pulling away the ethereal shroud that's surrounded the Utilidor for ages! Okay, maybe that's a little too much. Yes, a series of tunnels run under the Magic Kingdom, and they are called the Utilidor.

That's where our orientation tour began. It made sense, of course, as the Utilidor is where we would start each day and then walk to our respective "land" where we worked. So, it definitely helped with familiarization.

As a frequent previous Walt Disney World Guest did I find this somewhat off-putting? Oh yeah. After years of walking through the turnstiles, under the train station at the entrance, into Main Street U.S.A., and on to Cinderella Castle and the other lands, this was like walking into your house through the back door...in the basement...and then up a set of stairs... through a secret door...to your home that you've never entered.

As alien as this all felt, the team that created the orientation for the Magic Kingdom knew how important it was for me and all the other new Cast Members to become comfortable with the Utilidor and other "backstage" areas, as this was going to be a significant part of our world, working in the Magic Kingdom.

Another major part of our role was ensuring that the Guests' Walt Disney World experience was completely immersive. As Randy guided us all through the different lands of the Magic Kingdom, we learned about each land's stories and details. With that, we learned how, as Cast Members, we support that story, and the Show, through our roles.

Although we may be stocking shelves with plush toys, serving French fries, or asking Guests, "How many are in your

---

[4] Dave Smith, *Disney A to Z: The Disney Encyclopedia*, (New York, Disney Editions, 2006), p.706

party?" as they board an attraction vehicle, the Guests are in the midst of an experience, and all that we did and said needed to support that experience.

A greeting of "Howdy!" when entering Pecos Bill's Café in Frontierland or "Welcome Back, galactic travelers!" when exiting Space Mountain may seem like small, almost forced, touches, but as we learned in "Once Upon a Time…Is Now," it's a finishing touch and can be traced back to Walt Disney and his vision for what would make his theme park so different.

My Disney-obsessed head was spinning as I left orientation that day. As I walked to my car in the parking lot, I was swimming in enthusiasm and eagerness to get started as a Cast Member. My Main Street costume (not uniform) with its turn-of-the-last-century checked brown plaid vest, cream-colored shirt, and paisley tie, no doubt made me like look like an out-of-place extra from *Hello Dolly*, but even that couldn't dampen my spirits.

I couldn't wait to get up the following day, put on my costume (pray that I had checked out the right size), and get back to the Magic Kingdom. Good thing I felt this way because the next day was my first day of on-the-job training.

The rubber was about to hit the road, or, at least, my comfortable, black athletic shoes were about to hit the street.

My trainer Anne seemed to have a handle on everything. I felt like I had a handle on nothing; I was in awe. It was as if she had a superhuman ability to multitask that I was discouragingly sure I would never master.

I would be working in a shop called "Exposition Hall," which was a turn-of-the-last-century-like name for the Magic Kingdom Camera Center (all those years ago in 2000 when people still used these things called cameras).

The shop sold film, disposable and digital cameras and also provided a service for Guests to develop their film on *the same day*! (And an entire generation just asked, "What was *all that*?").

Long before today's PhotoPass service at Walt Disney World, where Guests can receive all their pictures digitally, Exposition Hall was where Guests picked up hard copies of photos that Disney Photographers took in front of Cinderella Castle and

Mickey's Toontown Fair (again, another generation just asked "Where was *that*?").

As we walked through the Utilidor, Anne asked me, "Do you know about cameras?"

"Ummm...I like to...take pictures," I said. Meanwhile, in my mind, I was anxiously saying, *"Anne! I know nothing! Please don't leave me!"*

I was nervous as we made our way through the Utilidor, and I continued to wonder if my costume fit correctly (it didn't, but that would come in time). I tried desperately to pay attention to the winding corridors, thrilled to finally see a sign that read "Main Street, U.S.A." with an arrow. If nothing else, I knew I could just look for that sign...but where was it again?...well, I could ask someone...but who? Ok, Pain and Panic were paying another visit.

Anne and I continued to talk as we made our way up some stairs and through doors into the daylight, walked past a parking lot, and then around a wall. And there was Main Street, U.S.A. We didn't enter through the main entrance; we entered between the Main Street Confectionary (the candy store) and Tony's Town Square Café (an excellent *Lady and the Tramp*-themed Italian restaurant).

All of a sudden, the sounds, the music, the smells, and the Guests were all there. I stopped in my tracks, and Anne said to me, "You okay?" All I could say was, "I feel like I just walked into my house through a window." She smiled, "Weird, isn't it?"

After that, the next two days were a blur of introductions to fellow Cast Members, processing transactions and introductions to Managers. Then, there were tours of stock rooms, how to find a product that's in the stock room, and introductions to more Cast Members. Then, there was a trip to the cafeteria (called the "Mouseketeria"), more introductions to Cast Members and Managers (thank God everyone was wearing name tags!).

Through it all, I would love to tell you I was stellar. I had left Merchantainment class several days before with an "I-got-this" cockiness of someone who clearly understood the difference between a multi-tender transaction and which of the two credit card slips the Guest should receive. I was *so* ready; I *so* had this; I was *so* delusional.

One day during training, for example, after Anne had processed several transactions and a Guest approached us wanting to buy a photo frame, Anne turned to me as we walked the Guest to the register and said, "You want to take this one?" *"Not really,"* I thought, but it came out as "Sure."

I stepped behind the register, and the Guest noticed the "Earning My Ears" ribbon hanging from the bottom of my nametag. The small fabric ribbon is given to all Cast Members during their training to denote, in a themed manner, of course, that they're in their first days. After training, it comes off (although some Cast will attempt to leave them on for months after, as a security blanket. But, when the ribbon gets worn and the sun fades it, people catch on!).

The Guest gestured to my ribbon and said, "Oh! You're in training!" I tried to smile and nod while attempting to remember my sign-in number for the register. And, I did remember it, and I signed in…and then a tumbleweed blew through my mind…and I forgot everything else that follows. It was as if Merchantainment had never happened.

Anne quickly jumped in and talked me through all the steps, which promptly came back, and, thankfully, the Guest paid cash, which just seemed like the easiest form of payment to process (none of that "high-tech" credit card swiping for me, just yet, please). And the next thing I knew, it was over. I felt like I had been pushed through a revolving door and emerged on the other side, handing the Guest a receipt.

And, the Guest couldn't have been sweeter, "You did great!" she assured me, as she chatted some more before wishing me good luck and leaving.

At the end of the two days, candidly, I didn't feel like I was doing great. It was two days of ups and downs; for every transaction that would go smoothly, there would be something else I couldn't quite grasp, such as where to find something in the stock room or even finding the stock room itself.

There were also a lot of other aspects of Exposition Hall, such as how to print out the pictures that the Guests were picking up and how to process the film they were dropping off to be developed. There was even a photo studio area, where we took pictures of the Guests that were superimposed into scenes with the Disney characters.

But, I had been to college, I worked for seven years as a writer, I could do impressive things like, I don't know, change a lightbulb and tell you who won the 1990 Best Picture Oscar (*Dances with Wolves*).

Why was all of this seeming so difficult and overwhelming? Because it was like the first day of school all over again. *Everything* was new. And, no matter who you are and what you've experienced, it can seem complicated and overwhelming whenever something is new, and you've never experienced it.

Add to that, this is now your job, at a place you've always wanted to work, and you just relocated 1,200 miles for it, and the weight of that gets a lot heavier.

Anne could sense this and proceeded to give me what may have seemed to her as a standard pep talk that she had probably given numerous times to other new Cast Members, but her words were new to me and rang true.

As we walked back through the Utilidor, in one sentence, she said something that not only provided the boost I needed, but it's something that's always stayed with me.

"Remember," she added, "*everyone* has a first day."

And I knew what she meant: it's ok to be new, it's ok to admit what you don't know, it's ok to ask for help. As simple as it may seem, all of that helps you someday become "the veteran" yourself.

Soon, I was working at Exposition Hall with a casual familiarity that seemed so foreign to me on that first day. I never got cocky (it's tough to swipe a credit card through a register with an impressive flourish), but I became comfortable.

I learned so much from Anne (who would come back to check in and see how I was doing) and Randy, Penny, and Brian during that first week with Walt Disney World. I learned how to learn, and more importantly, I learned the empathy and patience that comes with teaching others.

As more new Cast Members began their journeys after me, I found that I could relate and wanted to help improve their experiences (*Everyone has a first day*). As I was just about getting ready to celebrate one year with Walt Disney World,

I was asked by a manager if I would like to be a trainer. I thought, "Wait. What? I feel as if I just figured out where to store my lunch in the break room, and you want me to show other people what to do?"

I became a trainer, guiding new Cast as I had been just a year before, and it led me down a new path, not just at Disney but in my life. As I write this, I apologize to all of my teachers throughout the years; for not doing my homework and for saying that I hated you while commiserating around the cafeteria table with my fellow sixth graders: you were all right, you were all doing the right things for us and, looking back, all that you taught us is so important.

I write that because, thanks to Disney, I developed an appreciation for teaching and, in this case, training. Thanks to the leaders who had faith in me, I did become a trainer in my area, passing on my vast twelve-month knowledge of Exposition Hall to new Cast Members.

This led me down another path and, a year later, I auditioned to be a facilitator for Merchantainment class. However, I was sure I had blown the audition and would receive a complete set of Merchantainment trading cards as a consolation prize; but, no, I made it on to the team of facilitators.

I soon found myself in the classroom fashioned like a merchandise shop at Disney University, teaching new Merchandise Cast Members how to navigate the uncharted territory of a register and very much relating to the uber hesitation of even touching the keypad.

And then came a true-full circle moment, the following year, when I was able to join the Traditions Team. After another audition that I was sure would provide me a one-way ticket to the exit of Disney University, I found myself teaching the first-day orientation class at Walt Disney World. I had never thought, in any of my wildest dreams, when I sat in Traditions nervously, just three years prior, that I would be standing in front of classrooms full of, at times, seventy new Cast Members and about to introduce them to Walt Disney World.

The impact of this would be felt for me several months after I started teaching the class. I was visiting a friend who was staying at Disney's Yacht and Beach Club Resorts. As I walked into the lobby, a Valet Cast Member called, "Michael! Hey! Michael!" It turns out it was a Cast Member who had been in one of the Traditions classes I had taught and wanted to come over and say "Hi."

For me, it not only felt great, but it was significant in just how essential those early days at any job are and how a positive experience can last for some time.

"The Circle of Life" continued as I would segue into a leadership position as Merchandise Training Manager back at the Magic Kingdom. In fact, I began this role six years to the day that I started with the company.

I learned so many valuable lessons from my early days at Disney. There were things that I feel I innately knew and were in the back of my mind, but my experiences there highlighted them as never before.

From Traditions to Merchantainment to Once Upon a Time to on-the-job training, I had quite the first impression at Walt Disney World. It got me thinking about other "first days and weeks" at different jobs and how that wasn't always the case. I recalled applying for a job as an usher at a local multiplex in high school. After not introducing himself, the manager handed me my usher uniform (that didn't fit), letting me know that I should show up later that night and they "would figure out what they would do with me." I showed up later that night, all right, to turn in the ill-fitting polyester suit and clip-on tie and let them know it wasn't for me.

We've all had experiences like that with new jobs; we may still have them today. Disney made me realize how different those first days can be. When real-time is taken to immerse an employee in their new workplace, about the values of the company that they will be working for, about the expectations of their role, how to carry out those expectations and resources that are available, I was able to see first-hand, just how invaluable that time truly is.

And also, how overwhelming training and the first days on the job can be. Disney made it seem a lot less overwhelming. By starting with the "big picture" of Traditions and narrowing training down to what you will be doing (Merchantainment) and where you will be doing it (Once Upon a Time and on-the-job training), it was all so much easier to take in in its smaller doses (Sure, place the "Spoonful of Sugar" song right about here).

I also saw how patience and understanding by a trainer can get passed on to their trainee, who then bring it to all they do daily.

Those first days as a new Cast Member and that time as a trainer were as valuable as gold. Another well-worn saying has unfortunately made its way throughout many corporate communities: "What if we train them, and they leave? What if we don't train them, and they stay?"

The quote says so much. Yes, training is an investment and an incredibly significant one. During my first week and my time later working in training, I saw first-hand just how much Disney valued training and how important those first few steps and those that provide them are.

It's something that stays with me to this day; whether explaining something new or learning something new, the foundation of training I learned at Disney is still a part of me.

For me, back in October of 2000, two decades with Disney were about to start. And, like any great Disney attraction, it would be filled with some unexpected twists and turns, scary moments, laughter, the thrill of being on it with those who would become dear friends and the exhilaration of a ride unlike any other.

We start this ride, by turning the "Keys" to success!

CHAPTER THREE

"Four" Score

Safety, Courtesy, Show & Efficiency

Go to YouTube, and in the search bar, type: "Parents surprise kids with a trip to Walt Disney World." Go ahead. I'll wait.

Incredible, right? You probably just went down several hour-long "rabbit holes" of watching all those videos. In each one, parents find creative ways to surprise their children with the news that they are about to take a Walt Disney World vacation.

The children have no idea. They are ready for the news that they are doing something much more "mundane" in the realm of "kid-dom" when the parents inform them that, nope, they are going to Walt Disney World on vacation, right then and there. The reactions are amazing.

Children cheer, and some start crying, so overcome with emotion at the thought of going to this place that seems, quite literally, like a "World" away. Their reaction is sheer, unadulterated joy. Even the most cynical cynic, who sneers at a sunny day, can't help but get caught up in the sheer happiness of these videos.

It takes a lot for parents to plan these surprises. Heck, it takes a lot to plan a Walt Disney World vacation. Have you ever done it? These vacations are usually plotted like a strategic intercoastal crossing, mapped out years in advance, with a date on a calendar that seems never to get closer and a countdown that goes on forever.

As day one of the Walt Disney World vacation arrives, excitement builds faster than the humidity of a Florida summer.

Disney's marketing team knows this oh-so-well. A television commercial campaign entitled "Too Excited to Sleep" centered on a brother and sister who are so excited about their Walt

Disney World vacation that they can't sleep the night before (admittedly, the parents, at the end of the commercial, are too excited to sleep, too). Without a doubt, a direct reflection of the consumer. There are months of thoughts, possibilities, and shifting dates on a calendar, along with, let's face it, a good amount of money being spent, that goes into a Walt Disney World vacation.

For many, this could be their first, fiftieth, only, or sadly, their last visit to the "Vacation Kingdom of the World." So, what does this mean for Cast Members?

No pressure.

There's a lot to deliver for every Walt Disney World Guest. And, if you think planning to *come* to Walt Disney World can be a little overwhelming, try planning for everyone to *arrive* (just a small get-together with thousands of your closest friends about to show up).

So, how do Cast Members prepare for this?

By prioritizing through the Four Keys, as they were introduced when I attended Traditions:

- Safety
- Courtesy
- Show
- Efficiency

As stated, this was before the addition of Inclusion, which has always been a priority at Disney, as the fifth key.

Safety is first and foremost for Guests visiting Walt Disney World as well as the work environment for the Cast. It becomes the first filter for all decisions.

Courtesy is what Disney is world-renowned for, what Guests remember most about their experiences, and what other businesses try to emulate. Traditions teaches the first steps to provide this exceptional service by considering Courtesy in all Cast Members do.

Show supports the story being told in each park, resort, and other locations at Walt Disney World. Again, as it is a theme park, Traditions provides information on how to keep that theme a part of all that Cast Members do, from the costumes that are worn to greetings that are used and how cleanliness is essential for the stage that all Cast will be performing their roles on.

Efficiency teaches Cast Members how to perform all the other three Keys in the most effective manner. Guests love to take their time at Walt Disney World, so Cast Members need to help Guests make the most of that time, while performing their Cast Member roles in the most expeditious manner that's also safe, courteous, and supports the Show presented to the Guest.

As the Keys serve as pillars for the experience Disney provides for Guests, it's important to go through each one in detail:

Safety is the first of the Keys discussed in Traditions, as it is Disney's number one priority. Guests come from all over the globe to Walt Disney World for various reasons knowing that it is safe. Guests don't even think about Safety when riding an attraction, a monorail, or returning to their resort room at the night's end, they just know and feel that Walt Disney World is a safe place.

But, like everything else, that Safety takes a tremendous amount of work. In addition to an entire Security team found in all Walt Disney World areas, Cast are taught from day one that Safety is *everyone's* responsibility.

From making sure that "wet floor" signs are quickly placed in merchandise shops as soon as rain begins, to swiftly cleaning up a spilled drink on a restaurant floor, to ensuring that Guests are secure inside an attraction ride vehicle, there's not a part of the Walt Disney World experience that doesn't require Cast Members being trained in creating a safe experience.

Much like everything else, this experience is such that Guests don't even notice that their safety is being taken care of at every turn. Disney has a reputation for keeping Guests safe as their first precedence, even if it means that the experience may be disrupted.

Anyone who can recall a Walt Disney World visit during thunderstorm season knows that you won't be able to ride Big Thunder Mountain during a storm (which also is true for a number of other attractions). You also won't be able to buy merchandise or food at an outside cart or swim at the pool at your resort. Due to potential danger, outdoor activities at these times are also closed.

Of course, this is disappointing, especially for children, but it's also completely understood, at least for adults. Weather is watched very closely by the leadership teams at Disney, with the skill and precision of trained meteorologists, every day, for this reason.

These are just some of the many ways Disney looks out for every Guest's Safety.

At the same time, Disney is also committed to creating a safe environment for Cast Members. Traditions discusses how Cast Members cannot only assist with creating a safe workplace, but they learn that it is their role to keep Safety as part of the *culture* at Disney.

Though the Walt Disney World Resort is indeed that mecca where so many come to escape the realities of the real world, sometimes, with so many streaming through the turnstiles of the theme parks and staying at Disney resorts, accidents and illnesses are bound to happen.

Traditions training teaches Cast Members what to do in these situations. This starts with the fact that 911 should be called first in a situation involving a Guest illness or injury, even before a leader is called (Safety is the priority, after all, and a paramedic can assist more than, say, a manager of a restaurant). After 911 is called, of course, the leaders should be made aware.

In the class, Cast Members are taken through the steps of these situations, including how to provide the correct information to 911 and how to keep a Guest, and their family or friends, calm in these situations.

Yes, preparedness and the concept of Safety as the "first and foremost above all" stays with you as a Cast Member.

For example, in 2019, almost two decades after attending Traditions, I worked in a Proprietor role with the merchandise team at Disney's Hollywood Studios. I was leading a team of Guest Experience Managers and Cast Members, and we were responsible for operating several merchandise shops in the park.

When I first arrived at the park in early 2019, we were preparing for the highly anticipated opening of the new land, Star

Wars: Galaxy's Edge. Have you heard of it? Yeah, so has everyone else in the galaxy. As such, the incredibly immersive area was, to put it mildly, eagerly anticipated by *Star Wars* fans, Disney devotees, and theme park enthusiasts before its release.

Our team wasn't going to be directly responsible for the merchandise locations in Star Wars: Galaxy's Edge. Still, as the opening day in August that year moved closer, all teams in the park were brought into planning meetings. As the new land would be so popular, it was bound to impact the entire park.

There was talk of record-breaking attendance and that Guests would begin arriving *well* in advance of the opening of Star Wars: Galaxy's Edge. This fan base would be more than willing to come early, stay late and wait around all day, or days, to be among the first to experience Galaxy's Edge. If you've gone to one of the recent *Star Wars* films on opening weekend or engaged in discussing the latest *Star Wars* series on Disney+, you know that they can be as passionate as Boba Fett in search of his bounty.

The planning meetings I was a part of focused on effectively operating the park when a queue line of Guests just waiting to get *into* the new *Star Wars* land could wind and stretch throughout it. When discussing where the line would go or a waiting area would be staged, Safety was the first "filter" everything passed through.

Another consideration was that the opening would happen at the peak of rising temperatures in Florida. For me, it's only a slight exaggeration when they say that being in a Florida summer is akin to spending time on the sun's surface. There's a reason that Miami's basketball team is dubbed the "Heat!"

Many Guests who come to Florida from cooler climates aren't prepared for that kind of weather. As a Cast Member, one of the unfortunate, almost daily occurrences on a summer day is that Guests often succumb to the heat, feeling ill, or even passing out.

What to do when Disney's Hollywood Studios is bursting at the seams with Guests, many of whom may have similar heat-induced reactions, as "Galaxy's Edge" opens?

The answer was Safety. Umbrellas would be strategically placed throughout the park to provide ample shade, and complimentary water stations would also be available throughout the park to provide sufficient opportunity for Guests to stay hydrated.

Every time there was a discussion of moving a queue line of Guests, not just for Galaxy's Edge, but for purchasing food, merchandise, or other areas of the park, the Safety and comfort of the Guests was the first talking point. If the line was blocking an entrance or exit or creating a "bottleneck" of Guest traffic, and the Safety of the Guests couldn't be guaranteed, another option was considered.

Just as we looked to create that safe environment for Guests, Safety also becomes a piece of a Cast Member's role and performance as they interact "backstage" and with each other. It is part of a Cast Member's performance, and it is ingrained as Walt Disney World language.

Safety becomes that first thought for stock rooms, kitchens, break areas, and the like.

This Key is proactively creating a Safety plan before an incident occurs. Most of these plans revolved around small changes that could be made to avoid significant incidents down the road. One example I had seen around this involved stock room doors in the merchandise shops. Most doors open in, which could cause an accident if a Cast Member entered as another exited.

Two straightforward solutions surfaced. One was to place yellow caution tape on the floors of stock rooms to denote a "Please Do Not Stand Here" space. This became such a part of everyday life in merchandise that Cast Members would hold each other accountable, reminding their peers to step out of the taped space if they happened to forget (another example of how Safety becomes part of the culture).

Another solution, and a very simple one, was that Cast Members would knock on a stock room door before entering as a "warning" to those inside that the door was about to open. It took just a few seconds, but that's all that's needed to stay safe.

This concept starts with Traditions and the conversation around Safety in class. Cast are taught that they are responsible for their Safety, their peer's Safety and Guest Safety.

The continual learning around Safety continues for Cast Members, not just on day one but several months into their career. After being in their role for about a month, Cast are trained in additional safety techniques to help them perform their role better and avoid injuries.

This next class demonstrates how Cast can safely lift boxes and other heavier items (such as suitcases for those in bell services). It also assists Cast who do things repetitively in their role, something as small as squeezing the pump of a spray bottle over and over, and how doing this properly can assist with avoiding wrist and hand injuries.

This training class is full of small "light bulb moments" of how we rush or "force ourselves" to do certain things and how doing that can result in that small "twinge" of pain in the back, or worse.

The training even has implications outside of work. I've never lifted bags of groceries out of my car the same way since. In the process, I've broken fewer eggs or, more importantly, dented fewer boxes of Cap'n Crunch.

Just as Traditions was the foundation for a Cast Member's first day, Safety is the foundation for every day after. Cast come to understand that only by being safe is everything else possible. And only by creating and maintaining a safe environment will Cast Members be able to deliver upon the next Key: Courtesy.

The conversation around this key in Traditions revolves around the experience that Cast Members provide Guests and the service they deliver. Courtesy is something that Disney is world-renowned for and many other companies from around the world, from factories to hospitals, with some of the biggest corporate names behind them, come to study and bring back what they've learned to their own businesses.

And on day one, in Traditions Cast Members learn how this is done with one key phrase: "We create happiness." Now, their role may differ depending on where they work and what they do, but this approach remains the same. The entire phrase is, "We create happiness by providing the finest in entertainment, for people of all ages, everywhere."

It's a Cast Member's purpose. And while Traditions discusses it in the larger picture, the idea of "We create happiness" is both an easy *and* logical way to deliver on Courtesy for Guests.

Traditions teaches Cast Members that while Guests enjoy the bigger, more noticeable things at Walt Disney World, such as meeting their favorite characters, watching fireworks, and enjoying parades, it's often the smaller, quieter moments that are most impactful. In fact, Disney receives ongoing communication from Guests discussing how a Cast Member positively impacted and many times "saved" their vacation and experience at Walt Disney World through Courtesy.

What does Courtesy look like?

Well, to start, Traditions teaches that a greeting, a conversation, or a question can make a difference for a Guest and lead to a positive experience. The class also teaches how Cast can change everything for a Guest by just taking a few extra minutes to listen and then act to resolve a situation.

One example used in class is what happens if a Guest drops their ice cream cone. You, as a Cast Member, have the ability, even if you don't work in food and beverage, to take that Guest over to the nearest ice cream cart, or ice cream parlor and partner with a fellow Cast Member there to make sure that the Guest receives a replacement.

In fact, we would see something very similar happening in merchandise. One of the more popular items is the autograph book and pen sold in most shops. While working at a shop in what was once known as Future World at Epcot, a frantic mom rushed in to ask if we sold autograph books and pens. A Cast Member walked her over to the autograph books, and then the register, and as the Guest hurriedly looked for her wallet, she expressed concern.

That was because Figment, from the attraction Journey Into Imagination, was appearing right outside the shop, taking pictures and signing autographs (doesn't that purple dragon with the yellow sweater do wonders to warm your nostalgic Disney heart?!).

Figment was just outside, but the mom that came into the shop was frantic that she wouldn't be able to pay for the autograph book and pen to get out there in time. The Cast Member told the mom to go ahead and take the book and pen out to get the picture and that she could come back after to pay for it.

She looked at us, stunned, and when the Cast Member confirmed that it was okay and you saw the realization on her face that she wasn't going to be "swarmed and tackled" by Disney police, she thanked us, looked relieved and quickly made her way outside.

About fifteen minutes later, she returned with her son to thank us again and to pay for the autograph book, asking her son to thank us, as well.

Were we taking a chance that the Guest could have just kept going about her day without paying for the autograph book? Sure. In the grand scheme of things that day at Epcot, if the Guest would have walked away with the autograph book and pen, would that have mattered compared to being courteous to a family and making their day better? No, and that's no figment of your imagination. This type of Courtesy happens every day at Walt Disney World.

Cast know when they leave Traditions class that they are empowered to make these decisions. If something is easily "fixable" for a Guest, they can fix it. And, if that pen they're using for autographs from the characters runs out of ink? No need to show us the receipt or process a return; the Guest is simply given a new pen.

Now, of course, the recovery and reimbursement need to be equitable and make sense. It can't look like this: The pen that they're using for autographs from the characters has stopped working? Here is a week-long stay at Disney's Grand Floridian Resort and Spa.

As with Safety, Courtesy as one of the Keys is another filter that the Cast uses to provide those small and not-so-small moments. These moments create lasting memories for the families who have been waiting and saving for years to come to Walt Disney World.

We will get more into the detail around the impact that outstanding service can have, and how Disney provides it, in the next chapter.

For Guests, the idea of Cast Members demonstrating this Courtesy is as much a part of the experience of a Walt Disney World visit as having the theme to "It's a Small World" echoing through their heads for weeks after they return home.

Yes, it's all part of the Show, which is the next of the Keys. Since Cast Members are essentially performing each day, in every role, their stage is their location, and, as such, they must ensure that they are effectively performing their role in the Show.

Have you ever been to the theater? Maybe even to Broadway? Imagine sitting in the first row of a Broadway show, opening night, (I know, it's close to impossible to get tickets like that, but bear with me).

The glorious opening number begins, and just as it builds to its crescendo and the music swells, an actor stops, looks out into the audience, right where you're sitting in and says, "Hi mom!"

The woman seated next to you starts waving back, nudges you, and proudly says, "That's my son!"

It kind of takes you out of the moment, doesn't it? It essentially ruins the show for you and the entire audience. It would have been better if the actor performing stayed in character, played his part, and said "Hi!" to his mom *after* the show, when she visited him backstage.

Knowing their role, and playing it well, is also the responsibility of Cast Members at Walt Disney World, as well. This is how they preserve the Show.

Now, of course, Walt Disney World may be miles away from Broadway in New York City, but Cast Members are also in a Show, and everything they do makes sure that the Show can—and must—go on.

When working as the Magic Kingdom Merchandise Training Manager, for example, a Cast Member who worked in the shops in Adventureland epitomized the commitment to the Show. His name was Bob, but everyone knew him as "Pirate Bob."

He accessorized his Pirates costume with a tri-corner hat, and from the second he stepped into the shop, throughout his entire shift, he spoke in "Pirate speak," with plenty of "Arghhs," and a spot-on Long John Silver imitation from *Treasure Island* that Guests loved. While processing a transaction at a register or stocking a shelf, he never once broke character. He was remarkable!

That's because he created happiness every day and understood his role in the Show. Guests interacting with him surely knew they were at the Pirates of the Caribbean shop in Adventureland.

Also, "Pirate Bob" added to the Show, never distracted from it—which is another critical responsibility of all Cast Members. Smartphones have become an integral part of our life, and while they are an essential Walt Disney World communication tool, managers will utilize them as needed. But they can also be one of the many "real-world" distractions that could ruin the Show for Guests. If you walk through Frontierland and see a Cast Member dressed in their cowboy or cowgirl costume, sitting on a bench talking on their phone, drinking a Diet Coke, and discussing how late they stayed out last night, well, it doesn't exactly say "Old West" now does it?

Cast Members hold the Show in their hands, and, in many ways, that responsibility is precious. Personal and work-related conversations are going to *have* to happen, but should that Guest who just escaped the Carnotaurus on the Dinosaur attraction have to listen to how you had a flat, spilled your coffee, or swerved to avoid an alligator on the drive to work that day? (All of those happened to me, just luckily not on the *same* day.) It doesn't exactly feel like a "Dino-Institute" appropriate conversation now, does it?

This is why, as Cast Members have learned on day one, there are "backstage" and "onstage" locations. Just like the actor performing on Broadway should have said "Hi!" to his mom backstage and performed his role onstage, Cast know to do the same.

Backstage is where conversations and discussions that wouldn't support the Show take place. This is where one would complain to their fellow Cast Members about the gator, as mentioned above, that stepped in front of their car.

This is also where Cast Members can have conversations with their leaders about specific topics that may clash with the Show, such as a concern or ideas around possible improvements. Backstage is also where the teams that provide support have their offices, such as staffing, finance, and training, just to name a few.

Backstage, Cast Members can access break areas, cafeterias, and even conference rooms, where everything from recognition to regularly scheduled meetings are held. It wouldn't look good to pull up a table and several chairs in front of Spaceship Earth at Epcot and discuss plans would it?

It's vital to make this delineation between backstage and onstage so all that everything a Guest sees in the Show on stage is that much more special for the Guest experience. As a Cast Member, it becomes second nature to understand that as soon as you walk through a door or around a corner on stage, you are part of the Show.

When Walt Disney dedicated Disneyland in 1955, part of his speech was: "Here age relives fond memories of the past... and here youth may savor the promise of the future..."[5] At the Walt Disney World dedication in 1971, Walt's brother, Roy O. Disney, called it "...a Magic Kingdom where the young at heart of all ages can laugh and play and learn—together." [6]

Essentially, the Disney brothers were saying that their theme parks would be a place where Guests could come to forget the "real world," at least for a short time. Let's face it, there's a lot of reality out there, and we all deserve a break from it occasionally.

A perfect example takes place in the queue lines for Disney characters in the parks, where Guests wait to meet and take pictures with their favorites. Cast Members are trained and understand that while onstage, these characters are in *no way* entertainment Cast Members performing a role; these are *the* Disney characters.

That is *the* Elsa from *Frozen*, *the* Baloo from *The Jungle Book*, and *the* Mickey Mouse.

And as Cast Members, this is incorporated into your language. When I worked as a manager in the UK Pavilion at Epcot, Winnie the Pooh would meet with Guests in an area of the Toy Soldier shop. When Pooh bear would have to go backstage, the character attendant would tell the Guests, "He's just going to get a smakerel of honey." Just a small touch (and a lot better than yelling "Break time!") that preserves the magic that Guests have come to experience.

---

5 Christopher Finch, *The Art of Walt Disney: From Mickey Mouse to The Magic Kingdoms*, (New York, Harry N. Abrams, inc. Publishers), p.404.

6 Jeff Kurtti, *Since the World Began: Walt Disney World The First 25 Years,* (Hyperion, New York), p.39.

As another example, while working at Exposition Hall during one of my first days with the company, the Seven Dwarfs appeared in a section of the shop. One day, when assisting a Guest at the register, they asked me how many Dwarfs there were at the Walt Disney World Resort. I replied, "Seven." He clarified that there were Seven Dwarfs at Exposition Hall, but how many at Walt Disney World, overall? "Seven," I answered again, explaining, "Sir, it's Snow White and the *Seven* Dwarfs." He nodded and smiled, in appreciation.

And, the Guests *do* appreciate this protection of the magic. It's the reason they come to visit. They can get reality elsewhere.

Also adding to this Show, to the performances of all Cast Members is how the stage is set.

Going back to Broadway and that opening night show. Imagine, once again, if just as the music builds to its crescendo, but before the actor says "Hi!" to his mom, napkins and paper plates blow across the stage.

Again, it would distract, wouldn't it? How the stage is set is as important as what is happening on the stage.

In addition to Courtesy, Walt Disney World is just as world-renowned for how clean they keep every inch of its resort. How does this happen?

Again, this begins in Traditions. As the conversation on Show occurs in class, the facilitator asks, "How many of you will be working in custodial?" Usually, a smattering of hands would raise. The facilitator would then ask again, "Wait...*how* many of you are working in custodial?"

The Cast Members, even on their first day, get it. Soon, every hand in the classroom is raised. That's right, *all* Cast Members work in custodial, and they are all responsible for keeping Walt Disney World clean.

That complete ownership starts on day one, Cast are taught that if they should see trash on the ground, such as a napkin, or an empty cup, they don't need to call or find a custodial Cast Member; they can just pick it up.

Cast are even taught an easy way to do this called "The Disney Scoop," which is a way to swiftly bend down and pick something up without losing a step. A more ergonomic advancement surfaced during my time at Disney. For lack of a better term, they were called "pickers." These devices, which are about the length of a cane, allow one to pick up trash without even bending over.

As a Cast Member, making sure that all was clean becomes so much a part of your every day that it's a common joke among them that on days off, they find themselves picking up trash at the supermarket, the movie theater, random parking lots, or even at your friend's house (and I'm still apologizing to my friends to this day).

And with Safety always a priority, if there's anything that shouldn't be picked up, Cast are instructed to contact the appropriate custodial Cast trained to handle these situations.

Also, like Safety, Walt Disney World cleanliness is a team effort that becomes part of the culture of Show.

It's then the Key, Efficiency, that wraps everything up. Those same Guests who captured their excited children on video with the announcement they were going to Walt Disney World have quite the schedule and are hoping to get it all in during their stay.

It's Disney's focus on Efficiency that will help them do that. Since opening in 1971, Disney has sought new ways to make the Guest experience more efficient. In its earliest years, Guests would have to purchase a ticket book and provide a separate ticket for each attraction.

This eventually gave way to a one-price ticket, which created efficiencies by Guests not having to fumble in their pocket for a ticket book and Cast Members not having to take the ticket at the attraction.

Then, as the resort grew to include four theme parks, and lines at the popular attractions would consist of a wait time long enough so that Guests could watch a Disney double feature (ok, maybe an exaggeration), there was the introduction of FastPass. These were paper tickets printed out at machines by the attractions, providing the Guest with a time to return when there would be a minimal wait.

These saved Guests a tremendous amount of time through the years. I didn't realize how much, until one time, I spent most of a day off at the Department of Motor Vehicles. I was instructed to take a number from the ticket machine when I came through the door and wait my turn. I believe they were currently assisting number 51, and I think the number I took was 7,648.

As I sat in the waiting room, a man beside me leaned over and said, "They need FastPass here." The term had become shorthand for not having to wait long for something. By the way, DMV now allows you to make appointments ahead of time (maybe it *is* their version of FastPass?).

As smartphones became part of our lives, FastPass transitioned to the My Disney Experience app and then another advancement came with Genie and Lightning Lane.

It's not just technology. Everything that Disney does each day brings Efficiency into consideration. For example, a queue line may be formed in a certain way to allow for an additional number of Guests; at night, after the fireworks finale, Guests are instructed to exit the park in a specific direction, to allow the flow of foot traffic through the park to move quicker (and to not overwhelm the monorail, Skyliner or buses waiting outside the gates). Guests can now bypass a check-in at the lobby of their resort, check in on their phone, and use their phone to open the door to their room.

For Cast Members, there were also always small, individualized touches that they could use to make the Guest experience more efficient. In merchandise, this involved something as small as unwrapping the plastic from an autograph book so that it was ready for the Guest to use, or, at Exposition Hall, the Guest would pay at the register and then pick up their photos at the end of the counter, which was not only easier for them but kept the lines moving.

Indeed, Efficiency very neatly wraps up all of the Keys. As Guests enter the parks, there is the need to enter through a bag-check area, which keeps them safe but is also arranged in a way to accommodate a large number of Guests efficiently; the Security Cast courteously greets and talks with the Guests as they enter; and finally, if there are any spills of drinks or trash on the ground, these same Cast Members also know to clean them up quickly, to keep things Show ready, and then return to bag check. It all comes together to make sure Guests get into the park efficiently, especially during a busy morning when something time-sensitive and exciting like a Disney character buffet filled with never-ending hash browns and the chance to take a picture with Mickey, is on the other end of bag check.

In fact, I saw an example of Efficiency as an encapsulation of most of the other Keys first-hand in 2016 when I was working as a Proprietor at The World of Disney merchandise shop at Disney Springs. In the fall of that year, Hurricane Matthew was headed toward Central Florida. As it approached, at one point, it was a Category Five, the strongest of all hurricanes. With Safety in mind, the leadership team at Disney decided to close Walt Disney World theme parks, water parks, and Disney Springs on the day Matthew was projected to make landfall.

Guests staying at Walt Disney World Resorts were instructed to remain in their rooms for an extended period. They would be provided with food and snacks during this time frame.

The day the storm was projected to visit Central Florida, Matthew decided to do what many hurricanes have done through the years: completely change its mind. The hurricane veered away from Florida, stayed over the water, and began heading north.

Needless to say, there was complete relief (as well as an overstock of bottled water, batteries, and canned goods at my house). But, as the day continued to be filled with just cloudy skies, mild wind, and intermittent rain, there was also a concern among Walt Disney World Leadership.

With all of the theme parks and water parks closed on a day when they could be operating, there were now over thirty Walt Disney World Resort Hotels occupied with Guests who had been holed up in their rooms, filled with a lot of pent-up energy.

As I sat at home, realizing I had moved all my patio furniture inside for no reason, my phone rang. My leader, Susan, was calling to inform me that a decision had been made to re-open Disney Springs that evening to provide all of those Guests (whose vacation plans had been shaken like an "Etch-A-Sketch") with an opportunity for something to do. We were all being called back to work.

As Disney Springs, comprised mainly of retail and dining, didn't have attractions that would take time to bring back "online," it would be the quickest to re-open, as well as the *only* location to re-open.

This was terrific news for those staying at a Disney Resort. For the team at Disney Springs, this meant that Disney Transportation buses would soon be dropping off about 100,000 Guests on our "front porch," all coming to see us.

World of Disney is indeed a big shop (in fact, it's the largest of all of Disney's merchandise locations, anywhere), and as we gathered for a pre-opening meeting, the team started talking about how Efficiency would drive everything that evening.

As we opened our doors, and Guests streamed in as if Black Friday had come early that year, they started to make purchases. The queue line at the registers began to grow past the designated area in front of the counter, spilling over into the rest of that room, then the next.

We knew we had to act. Cast Members were soon designated to direct the line so that it didn't interfere with the rest of the shop or impede the flow of traffic. Some even acted like "traffic cops," where there were "breaks" in the line, allowing Guests to keep shopping. Without this, not only would this have turned into a Safety issue, but there would have been no way to move the Guests efficiently through the store.

Additionally, all registers (and there are a LOT of them) in the store were open to ensure that the line would move efficiently. Further, this allowed the Guests to purchase what they needed and get on with the rest of their evening. Other shops, restaurants, and even the AMC movie theater were open, which meant *so* much to Guests who were captive in their resort rooms, watching either the hurricane coverage on the news or *Frozen* for the eighty-seventh time.

Cast were instructed to provide the usual, traditional service but not over-engage. "So good to see you tonight" and "So glad you could be with us" was much more appropriate than "How's your vacation?" First, that question would open up a potential can of not-so-fresh worms to Guests, after the storm that had thrown several monkey wrenches their way, and second, it could lead to a more extended conversation that would not only slow up the line of Guests who were waiting but also keep the Guests from enjoying the other offerings.

We all also wanted to avoid any impediments or hassles for the Guests, and we were committed to make things easy for them. One Guest wanted to return a Snow White costume they had purchased for their daughter to wear to "Mickey's Not-So-Scary Halloween Party," which had been canceled due to the hurricane.

She didn't have the receipt, and the tags had been removed. There was no hesitation; she was allowed to return it. And those situations of efficient service recovery happened throughout the night.

Efficiency quickly became Courtesy. The less time a Guest spent in line and the less time they had to wait for "approvals," the more it created a positive experience for them.

As these Guests continued to make purchases, the stock on the shelves dwindled. Bare shelves could be seen in many rooms throughout the World of Disney. Show was taking a hit.

The stock team quickly devised a plan that could have best been termed a "bucket brigade." And, instead of one or two Cast Members, there were multiple involved in that brigade. Some were assigned to pull what stock was needed from the stock room, and load it on carts, others were assigned to transport it in carts to a backstage location, and then several Cast would retrieve the carts and re-stock the shelves in the store, just as another Cast Member brought out another cart loaded with merchandise.

It was an efficient way to preserve the Show.

While that evening would be hectic and a bit of a "blur," it was also gratifying. Guests patiently waited in the long lines, and so many made time to thank us all for being there and "saving" their day. And that thanks was much appreciated, as we had all left our homes and families at the tail-end of a hurricane, after the stress that comes with preparing for the unknown, to come back in to work that evening.

Thankfully, we all came together, as all the Keys came together perfectly, that day.

That's just one of the many days that taught me valuable lessons, thanks to the Four Keys. The Keys are an ideal example of how to set expectations for employees, or, in this case, Cast, and how these expectations should be filtered. Working at Walt Disney World can be overwhelming, and it's always more than comforting to have a "true North" on your compass to turn to when making decisions, creating a process, or venturing into anything new.

That's what the Keys provide. They were also a lesson in what the values of Disney were and how they were prioritized.

As Safety is the first Key, it spoke volumes about what Disney spotlighted and what should be the first thought in any meaningful conversation. Courtesy is a constant reminder of what Guest expectations are and what they represent. Show always reminds one to be aware of their surroundings and their appearance. Efficiency is the reminder that there is always a better way to do something.

With the addition of the fifth key, Inclusion, the Four Keys is also a lesson in how to set a vision for employees. As Cast could always treat them as a guidepost from day one, the Keys are also the reminder that Safety, Courtesy, Show, and Efficiency aren't just one person or team's responsibility. The Four Keys always reminded me that *everyone* owns *everything*.

And with this shared responsibility came a lesson in accountability and pride in all corners of what one does.

These Keys are also an important cue to always consider the Guest experience. All of those "Parents surprise kids with a trip to Walt Disney World" videos didn't show one thing—the families returning home, their exuberance a little lower.

Those families, like many, as they proceed to wash seventeen pounds of laundry and scroll through the forty-seven identical photos of Cinderella Castle on their phones, hopefully reflect on the unparalleled service they received during their visit and the Cast they encountered.

Guest service, and the stories (and, yes, magic) that come from that, is a point of pride for all in the Walt Disney World Cast and, as you're about to see, a hallmark of being a Cast Member.

CHAPTER FOUR

"Y'All Come Back, Ya Hear?!"
Guest Service

When I was managing the Walt Disney World shops at Orlando International Airport, there was a Cast Member who worked with us named Mickey. Yup, that was his name. Quite fortuitous that he worked for Disney.

At the time, this particular Mickey had been working for Disney for over two decades and brought with him energy that seemed like it was his first day. He was remarkable to watch as he interacted with Guests. As soon as any Guest was in his vicinity, Mickey would greet them and start a conversation, and with his gregarious sense of humor, the Guest would soon be laughing and feel welcome.

This was an innate skill that Mickey possessed. After watching him take time with a Guest one day, I asked him, "How do you do that?" He thought for a moment and responded, "Well, every Guest has a story. Our job is to find out what that story is."

At that moment, "our" Mickey perfectly encapsulated how to offer the outstanding service that inspire Guests to marvel (and I don't mean the superheroes).

The Walt Disney World shops at Orlando Airport were a unique experience for both Cast and Guest. They weren't located on Walt Disney World property. They were amid an international airport, which was a bustling, hectic, serious setting (one of the shops looked out on the TSA screening point, not exactly a sun dappled view of Cinderella Castle).

However, Mickey and all the Cast at the Disney airport shops made it feel like Walt Disney World within the walls of the shop, providing Guests who had just arrived in Florida with their first introduction to Disney and Guests who were getting ready to head back home with that last "taste" of the unique Disney magic.

The Cast at the Disney airport shops liked to call themselves "Disney Ambassadors," with pride, as they brought all that Guests loved about Disney to Orlando International Airport.

That role of "Disney Ambassador" is part of what each Cast Member does each day.

The Walt Disney World Ambassador is an *actual* role that's been a part of every Disney Park worldwide since the very first Disneyland Ambassador, Julie Reihm, in 1965. Every two years, the leadership team holds auditions and selects a Cast Member to represent the Park and Resort. Dave Smith, Director of The Walt Disney Archives, described the role in his book, *Disney A to Z*: "The ambassador travels to participate in parades, hospital visits, television and radio interviews, and other special events..."[7]

Not all Cast Members would have the opportunity to embark on such events, but all Cast would hold the similar responsibilities of representing Disney to Guests.

As stated in Traditions, this was done by "creating happiness," each day at Walt Disney World, and *this* was done through the service provided to each Guest.

The positivity, the kindness, and the "To infinity and beyond" (again, it's all about theming) that Guests receive at Disney Parks and Resorts stands out because it *stands out*.

About a year after moving to Florida, I went back to New York on vacation, to visit family. While there, I went to the grocery store with my dad. As we went to the checkout, the cashier never greeted my dad and instead just kept her head down and began scanning his items. When she finished, she hit the total but never even told the total to my dad. My dad looked at the register screen and handed the cashier his money. She took it and handed him back his change.

During all of this, I bagged my dad's groceries. My dad took his change, and we both left.

As we walked into the parking lot, I turned to my father and said, "The cashier never spoke to you." My Dad shrugged and said, "Happens there all the time. I am used to it."

---

7 Dave Smith, *Disney A to Z* (Disney Editions, NY, 2006), p.26.

And after about a year of working for Disney and being used to the service there, it was then that I realized we are all "used to" not receiving the level of service we receive at Disney when we go elsewhere.

There are wonderful, shining examples of service at locations beyond the berm of Walt Disney World Resort. This is why we are more likely to get our morning coffee, shop for our groceries, or even buy a car from these places that provide this service.

This is also why so many return to Disney and would rather vacation there for the one-hundredth time than go elsewhere for the first time.

So many have also asked "How does Disney provide such amazing service?"

Mickey (the Cast Member at the Airport shops, not the Mouse) provided the answer: "Every Guest has a story. Our job is to find out what that story is."

And that's the answer to the question so many ask.

But how do Cast Members discover that story?

That can be traced back to Disneyland's earliest days.

In his book, *Creating Magic: 10 Common Sense Leadership Strategies from a Life at Disney*, Former Executive Vice President of Operations, Lee Cockerell, discusses these early days when Walt set the standard. He writes:

"Back when Orlando was still a sleepy town, Walt Disney wrote the following to the leadership of his young theme park in Anaheim, California: 'Here at Disneyland, we meet our world public on a person-to-person basis for the first time. Your every action (and mine as well) is a direct reflection of our entire organization.' That spirit of purpose has been instilled ever since in each individual who works at what became the biggest resort business in the world."[8]

Different practices supported this during my two decades with Disney, but all had the original goal in place since Walt's time. As Cast Members, these became the air that we would breathe.

---

8 Lee Cockerell, *Creating Magic: 10 Common Sense Strategies from a Life at Disney* (New York, Doubleday, 2008), pp.118-119.

For several years, there were "The Seven Guest Service Guidelines:"

- Make Eye Contact and Smile.
- Greet and Welcome Each and Every Guest.
- Seek Out Guest Contact.
- Provide Immediate Service Recovery.
- Display Appropriate Body Language at All Times.
- Preserve the "Magical" Guest Experience.
- Thank Each and Every Guest.

And, in true Disney fashion, these would be themed around the Seven Dwarfs, making them easier to remember.

In addition to learning "The Seven Guest Service Guidelines" from day one, Cast are taught to treat Guests as a V.I.P., which here stands for Very *Individual* Person. Interactions are personalized, from noticing a character on a Guest's shirt, a young guest dressed as a princess, and Guests wearing "Celebration buttons."

For those who have never seen these pinback buttons, they are complimentary, at the Walt Disney World Resort and announce that a Guest is celebrating a special occasion. They can be personalized to let all know that the Guest is celebrating such occasions as birthdays, anniversaries, graduations, retirement, family vacations, first Walt Disney World visits, and so many other special days.

I met a Guest one day celebrating the fact that she was one-year cancer free, and she was very emotional when we congratulated her.

As the buttons could be personalized, I was able to be a part of a number of eclectic celebrations, meeting Guests with buttons announcing that they were celebrating everything from the last day of school to the first pumpkin spice latte of the season.

There were interactions like this each day at Disney and plenty of opportunities to make a Guest feel special.

In merchandise, we had plenty of chances for these personalized moments, particularly when a Guest handed you their credit card (*way* back in the day, prior to contactless payment, when they *did* give you their credit card). As you handed the card back to them, it was always nice to thank them and use the name you noticed on their card (plus, it was sometimes fun to see the reaction from their children, who wondered how in the heck you knew their parents).

Whether Seven Guest Service Guidelines, or Very Individualized Service, it all comes back to my co-worker Mickey at the Airport: "Every Guest has a story. Our job is to find out what that story is."

Sometimes, that story is *part* of the story or the experience. At Star Wars: Galaxy's Edge, the Cast undergo very detailed training to ensure that they are aware of the backstory of Black Spire Outpost on the planet of Batuu, where Galaxy's Edge is located. Their role is one of someone who exists in the *Star Wars* universe.

Much like "Pirate Bob" in Adventureland, the Galaxy's Edge Cast rarely steps out of character or the story, leading to some memorable Guest moments. One time, I was visiting the Park as a Guest with a friend who was wearing a Yoda T-shirt. A Galaxy's Edge Cast Member stopped and, instead of just commenting on what a great shirt it was, they exclaimed, "You have a shirt with the one and only Master Yoda on it? I have heard so many stories about him!" They then told us to be careful, as Stormtroopers in the area didn't take kindly to Jedi sympathizers.

Guests at Galaxy's Edge can also build their own Lightsaber at Savi's Workshop, which puts them into a moment where they are truly part of the *Star Wars* "show," complete with background music and a mystical conclusion. No spoilers here, but suffice it to say, it has been known to bring a tear to the eye of anyone who still has their *Star Wars* action figures "mint in box."

Even if you aren't a part of a story as rich as that in Galaxy's Edge, the wonderful part about working at the Walt Disney World Resort is that you are still a part of the story of Disney and have the ability to create an excellent experience for Guests through the service that you deliver.

While working at the *Dinosaur* shop at the attraction of the same name at Disney's Animal Kingdom Theme Park, we would greet Guests with, "Welcome back, time travelers!" While at Toy Story Land at Disney's Hollywood Studios, we would say, "Welcome to Andy's Backyard!"

How does this happen? In training, Cast Members are taught to initiate these interactions.

When Merchandise Cast Members aren't assisting a Guest at the register, they are trained to come out from behind the register and walk the shop, to interact with Guests, not wait for them to come to them.

When stocking the sales floor, which can be a very focused task, Cast Members should be aware of their surroundings and stop their task to assist Guests.

Pin trading is one of the most popular and important areas of merchandise as well as an opportunity for the Cast to exemplify great service. This began at the Walt Disney World Resort in 1999 for the Millennium Celebration and has proven so successful that it has continued since.

Inspired by pin trading at the Olympics, Disney employs the same method. Cast Members wear lanyards with Disney-themed pins on them. Guests can buy Disney-themed pins and then trade them one-for-one with Cast Members.

Have you ever collected…anything? Well, you can relate to Guests who collect pins and are always on the hunt for their "white whale" of a pin. And, as Guests sometimes wear their pins on multiple lanyards, baseball hats, and vests, you could usually spot a Guest interested in pin trading. With this, there was always an opportunity to interact with a Guest.

Other Guests might be on a mission and given an ultimatum to get into the shop, get what their looking for, and get back to their family (the next show of the American Adventure starts in five minutes, and it is not going to be a Disney vacation if you miss it!). A Cast Member approaches first so that Guests can get to the product they're looking for quickly and avoid a family argument in a situation like this.

A great time to have a Cast Member available walking throughout the shop was just as it starts to rain (which, in Florida, is scheduled almost as regularly as parades and shows). Guests immediately come in looking to purchase rain ponchos, which are available at the register. Having a Cast Member to direct them before they scour the shop in frustration is a small game changer.

When I worked as a manager at The Living Seas shop at Epcot, we would deploy a Cast Member to stand just outside the shop once we were aware of rain coming, with a cart full of ponchos to sell to Guests. It assisted the Guests with what they needed and allowed them to continue their day.

Sometimes this excellent service had nothing to do with the specifics of your role. Discussing that all Cast Members have a different role, but all have the same purpose: "We create happiness," means that sometimes Cast must step out of the parameters of their traditional role.

I saw this first-hand while still a brand-new Cast Member on Main Street, U.S.A. On a very busy Christmas Eve, a Guest came into Exposition Hall, distraught. While sitting on the curb watching the night time SpectroMagic Parade, they dropped a roll of film on the street. The canister of film then rolled backward and into the sewer.

Thankfully, we no longer have to worry about such tragedies today. Now, we just lose our entire phone.

The Guest asked if I could assist her, and my first thought was, "Gee, if you wanted to buy a roll of film, sure, but I left my waders at home. Otherwise, I would go tromping around the sewer."

Luckily, my manager Mike was there to answer, "Well, ya know, I work in merchandise, but I have no doubt I can find someone to assist you." Mike asked the Guests to show him where they were sitting, and since I was the one who got him into this, he asked me to come with them.

The Guest had been on the curb right in front of Exposition Hall, and a manhole cover was near where she was sitting. Mike quickly got on the phone with the Engineering team, and about fifteen minutes later, two Engineering Cast Members showed up with a crowbar and a flashlight. We cleared an area around the manhole (you know what will ruin your Christmas vacation to Disney? Falling into a sewer. Again, Safety first).

One of the Engineering Cast Members removed the manhole cover and clicked on their flashlight. I kid you not, right there, caught in the beam, was a roll of film, protected in its plastic case. The other Engineering Cast Member was able to use a tool to reach down and retrieve it.

The Guest started tearing up as the film was handed to her (no, there wasn't a pungent smell coming off it). She was grateful for all that had been done.

A Christmas miracle? Could be. Excellent service? Definitely.

Let's return to the Disney shops at Orlando International Airport. The role of the Cast Members was that of a Merchandise Host or Hostess but working at an airport meant sometimes going beyond that to assist a Guest.

An example of that, once again, involves our co-worker Mickey, who encountered a young Guest in the shop one day who was upset because they had left their favorite stuffed animal on Disney's Magical Express bus (the buses that shuttled Guests from the airport to their Disney resort, when they arrived and brought them back when they were departing).

The Disney's Magical Express team were excellent partners for the Disney merchandise team at the airport. As we were both operating "off property," both teams understood how we were "Disney outposts," of sorts, for the Guests.

As there was such a strong partnership, Mickey was able to contact the Magical Express team, which in turn, were able to contact the bus driver, who, in turn, found the stuffed animal and returned to the airport with it. The young Guest was emotionally reunited with his plush pal just before getting on his flight back home.

Cue the music—how's that for ending your Disney vacation on a high note?

These are examples of how discovering the "story" for these Guests truly turned everything around. No doubt, there were many times since when they have replayed the moment where their roll of film and stuffed animal were "saved."

I've thought about those moments since (and remember them vividly enough to include them here). I've often thought, "What if nothing had been done for those Guests? What if an apology was given, along with a 'really wish there was more that I could do?'"

How different the impact and the memories would have been.

That's a huge part of what Disney Cast Members do through the service they provide to Guests. Each opportunity to learn that Guest's story is an opportunity to make a change for the better for someone, no matter how small.

The concept of Cast Members making a difference has always been a part of the culture at Disney and was the centerpiece of a program I was fortunate to be a part of while working as the Magic Kingdom Merchandise Training Manager.

It was the introduction of "The Disney Service Basics," which stated:

I project a positive image and energy.

I am courteous and respectful to Guests of all ages.

I go above and beyond to exceed Guest expectations.

The overarching theme of The Disney Service Basics was: "I can make a difference for a Guest." The "I" in the language provided ownership to the Cast Member. Through additional training for all (no matter how long they had been with the company), Cast could see through their interactions that they genuinely could make a difference for Guests (whether retrieving film from a sewer or a stuffed animal from a bus).

This ownership and realization that "I can make a difference" is indeed the differentiator (it's right there in the statement) that lead to moments that changed the trajectory of a Guest's experience at Walt Disney World Resort for the better.

Letters, e-mails, and voice mails flood Disney's communication team, praising Cast Members. If they had background music swelling behind them, these Guest letters could serve as marketing that could lead many to plan their Disney getaway tomorrow.

But life isn't as perfect as a Walt Disney World commercial, and, unfortunately, not every Guest experience at Disney is perfect, either. For various reasons, some Guests experience difficulties (and some get out of control, Clark Griswold-style) that make for a less than a magical vacation.

When that happens, it's up to Cast Members to employ a different level of guest service, which helps recover what's been lost for the Guest.

In these situations, we would implement a service model called "L.A.S.T." This model wasn't developed by Disney and is well-known and utilized throughout the service industry. Disney has adopted it as the most effective way to turn that awful moment around and quickly diffuse a difficult situation.

The acronym stands for Listen (listening to the Guest's concerns), Apologize (letting the Guest know how sorry you are for what happened), Solve (coming up with a plan to solve the challenge and communicating that to the Guest), and Thank (making sure to thank the Guest for letting you know about the situation, and thanking them again as the situation resolves).

As an acronym, L.A.S.T. is easy and helpful to remember, especially when there's an angry Guest standing in front of you doing their best impersonation of Hades from *Hercules*.

I experienced this many times, and using this model was an extremely effective way to turn a challenging Guest situation around. One evening, working as a manager in World Showcase at Epcot, I was walking into one of our shops, and before I even stepped through the door on a beautiful Florida fall evening, I could hear a Guest shouting.

Now, even if you've never worked in the service industry, you probably know that this isn't a good sign, and, yes, when you hear that, part of you wants to turn around and be, well, anywhere but there, but situations like this are, unfortunately, part of the job.

The shop was the International Gateway shop (the small shop in the back of World Showcase, near the turnstiles that lead to Disney's Boardwalk and Yacht and Beach Club Resorts). In addition to selling merchandise, something offered in the shop was rentals of Electric Conveyance Vehicles (ECVs). These are small, single-rider, scooter-like vehicles made available for Guests with mobility challenges.

The high-decibel Guest I heard before I entered the shop had rented one earlier in the day and did not have a good experience (that probably explained the shouting). The first ECV he rented that morning lost its charge in the middle of the day. Cast Members were able to get a replacement ECV to the Guest, but the day that this happened was a Saturday, during the popular International Food and Wine Festival.

This meant it was crowded, *very* crowded. If you've been to The Epcot International Food & Wine Festival, you know it can make a Saturday in October feel like New Year's Eve. With this, it took some time for a Cast Member to bring the replacement ECV to the Guest, which meant the Guest had to wait.

Once the Guest had the replacement ECV, their day didn't get much better, and a snowball effect started. They were frustrated by navigating the vehicle through the crowd, and it was a perfect weather day, which meant it was sunny, hot, and sweltering in Florida.

As evening came, the Guest stated that the replacement ECV began to run slower and that it seemed as if it was, once again, losing its charge. They requested a replacement which once again meant that a Cast Member had to bring an ECV to them, which was, once again, delayed due to the crowd.

This time, however, the Guest was waiting on a dining reservation at the Biergarten restaurant in the Germany pavilion.

The snowball kept rolling down the hill, steaming in the warm sun.

By the time the ECV got to the Guest, they were late for their dining reservation (luckily, the Cast Member at the Biergarten worked fast and got them the following available table once the Guest got to the restaurant).

However, because they were late for dinner, they were in the restaurant when the Illuminations fireworks started and missed part of the show.

The snowball was on a roll now.

The family had also planned to shop in World Showcase after the fireworks. The only problem? All the shops in World Showcase closed when the fireworks started.

Rolling...rolling...and boiling!

One shop still open in World Showcase after fireworks was International Gateway, where this extremely frustrated Guest was headed.

The snowball was turning into an avalanche, of lava!

The Guest came into the shop and asked the Cast Member for a refund on their ECV. Now, it was the policy that ECV rentals are not eligible for a refund, and the Cast Member apologized and explained that to the Guest.

That's when I walked in.

The first thing I saw was not only a Guest shouting but also tearing up their ECV rental paperwork in front of the now shaken Cast Member, who was extremely happy to see me walk through the door.

I said hello and introduced myself to the Guest (they could have cared less that they were talking to Michael, they just wanted their money back, but introductions were still the right thing to do).

As the Guest was frustrated, they were getting loud. I asked if we could step off to the side, and even though I was remaining calm, my mind, much like the Cast Member, was reeling. But, like a beacon of hope, I could see the "L.A.S.T" model in my mind, blinking like a neon light.

I listened to the Guest tell me the entire story of a wearisome day. I *listened* and didn't just nod my head while thinking of what to do next. I could completely understand the frustration and had been a Guest at Disney on busy days while there with family and could imagine the time lost here, which was what the Guest was most upset about.

I then apologized. Many might think that by apologizing, you are "admitting fault," and in our litigious society could be opening yourself up for a legal issue. I didn't even think about being on the witness stand saying, "Yes, your honor, I *did* rent this Guest an ECV." You can't let yourself go down that paranoid road; you need to express your apology to the Guest.

I was simply letting the Guest know that I was sorry that this happened to them, which I was.

I then moved on to Solve and let them know I would process a refund for their ECV rental. I also told them that the Cast Member who assisted them was doing the right thing and following the correct process and that I would be making the exception. In situations like this, it was always important not to discount a Cast Member who was following the correct procedure, make sure that the Cast Member heard you, and that they know they aren't being discounted.

Then, knowing that so much time had been lost and that, at this point, the Guest wanted to get back to their Resort (Disney's Boardwalk Resort, which was next door), we partnered with

Guest Relations to have a Cast Member in a company vehicle drive the Guest and their family back to their resort.

We also learned that the Guest was planning a Disney's Animal Kingdom visit the next day, so we had Guest Relations get them a FastPass to use on an attraction there. As we waited for the Guest Relations Cast Member, we offered the Guest and their family some complimentary bottled water.

As the family left to get into the van with the Guest Relations Cast Member, the father (the flame emerging from his head now extinguished) shook our hands and thanked us.

We felt relieved and satisfied that we had taken a situation where a Guest had everything to complain about and left them with nothing to complain about (oh, sure, there was still the climate crisis, but that was out of our control).

Many may look at that situation and say, "But you broke the rules! And, you gave away free stuff!" True, but look what we gained: satisfied Guests who left feeling better than they had just a short while earlier. This moment might convince them to return. Disney is no longer just a "once and done" vacation, but a tradition (there's that word again); Guests return over and over again, sometimes each year, sometimes multiple times a year.

What's wrong with breaking a rule that won't get you arrested or fired? After all, at Disney, as it was said, "We Create Happiness."

Others might say, "What about people who take advantage? I have heard about people who go to, and return to, Disney specifically to take advantage and try to get as much as they can, for free."

Honestly, that wasn't too much of our concern as a Cast Member. Our job was to focus on creating that happiness. There were other teams at Disney, from Security to the Loss Prevention investigation teams that would investigate Guests who were focused on taking advantage.

Our role as Cast Members was to do what we could to make that day better for the Guests.

As leaders, it was also important to "walk this talk" regarding service. Managing the operation of an area of a theme park, or resort, or, really, any location at Walt Disney World, can make for a busy day and a head filled with distractions.

And while you may be focused on something as you make your way "onstage," you can't just walk by the Guest who is holding a guide map upside down and looking concerned. You need to stop and assist them, greet Guests, and interact, no matter how busy you may be.

During my Disney Springs days, I worked with a master of this art form: a Duty Manager named Lorraine. Duty Managers have a challenging role at the Walt Disney World Resort. They serve as the "overseer" for the park, resort, or water park, for which they are responsible, which in this case was Disney Springs.

They partner with leaders in all lines of business to ensure that all Four of the Keys—Safety, Courtesy, Show, and Efficiency—are happening as they should. They also deal with challenging situations and make sure that everyone, Guest and Cast, is safe and well taken care of. The Duty Manager looks at the operation wholistically, communicating any happenings at the property that they are responsible for to leadership and, as they spend most of their day walking the areas, they also calibrate Guest service.

As Lorraine would make her way through her day, with all these responsibilities on her plate, she would greet every Guest and Cast Member she encountered. It was an inspiration to see her skill at this, while multitasking all else she had going on.

She also never hesitated to step into any problematic situation and improve it. I observed her once talking with a Guest who had become quite upset and was, understandably, getting very vocal in the lobby of Guest Relations. The Guest was having ongoing, multiple challenges renewing their annual pass and had just hit another roadblock.

Lorraine oh-so-seamlessly employed the L.A.S.T model, adding a nice touch when it came to the Solve portion. She told the Guest, "*We* are going to solve this together." You could almost feel the temperature drop in the room. It was quite the message to the Guest, who now knew that Lorraine was *with* them until this situation was resolved, (and it eventually was for those of you at home concerned about the Guest's annual pass).

Through her actions, Lorraine was a great example to us when it came to Guest Service. I saw that this was critical for Guest Service to be effective. Like all areas of Leadership, it wouldn't work unless the leaders greeted and interacted with Guests and supported Cast Members by jumping in to resolve these difficult situations.

Cast needed to know that, as a leader, you were *with* them, together, just as Lorraine was with that Guest, and that the experience provided to Guests was *all* your responsibility. And as a leader, you would teach and mentor and, most importantly, recognize Cast Members when they provide outstanding service.

Recognition is so vital. Disney employed several recognition programs and was front and center in ensuring that Cast Members knew how appreciated they were. From large-scale parties to certificates presented to Cast, they were all wonderful and meant so much.

But, when these weren't available on a day-to-day basis, I found something that was just as powerful: a meaningful conversation with the Cast Member, thanking them for all they did for a Guest and letting them know how well they did.

Let's face it, we all like to hear a "well done" from the leaders in our life. However, it's more than just the feel-good boost. It also confirms that we are doing a great job and should continue down that path.

There's a reason someone invented applause.

While working as an Area Manager at Downtown Disney (now Disney Springs), we were having challenges with a Cast Member who wasn't greeting or even talking to Guests. As the leaders on our team spoke with him, we discovered he was very introverted, and it was sometimes difficult for him even to approach a Guest. The leaders worked closely with him, taking the time with him on stage to greet and talk with Guests (once again, leading by example).

Still, with all this time, when we would walk into the shop filled with Guests, the Cast Member was standing off to the side with great trepidation. We were all starting to feel very deflated by the situation.

One day, one of the leaders stopped me as I walked into the shop to let me know that the Cast Member had been by the door, greeting Guests and was currently talking to a family and trading pins.

I hurried off with them, and sure enough, there he was. Some switch of comfortability had been turned on within the Cast Member. As the family walked away, I said, "Well, let's go thank him."

As we talked with the Cast Member about what we observed and recognized him, there was a look of relief and appreciation on his face. What if we had done nothing? Or just nodded and walked away. All that time spent, particularly by the Cast Member, wondering if they were doing the right thing and doing it correctly would have been for naught, and maybe they wouldn't have done it again.

It just took a few minutes and a simple "Thank you."

Kindness, positivity, and treating others as you would like to be treated.

It seems simple, but that's the lessons learned when it comes to Guest service.

Kindness, when it comes to actively greeting Guests, anticipating their needs, empathizing, and assisting them during challenging situations.

Positivity is about creating an experience for the Guest, whether they are in Fantasyland at Magic Kingdom Park or the Fantasia shop at Disney's Contemporary Resort. It's also about reflecting what Disney stands for and means to the Guests who visit.

And treating others as you would like to be treated. If you've ever visited Disney or anywhere, and you and your family or friends were treated exceptionally well—look to return that.

As our airport friend Mickey said, "Every Guest has a story. Our job is to find out what that story is." That kindness, positivity, and treating others as you would like to be treated is how those stories are discovered.

And it's the reason so many Guests return to Disney. As they say at The Country Bear Jamboree, "Y'all come back, ya hear?!?"...and they do!

It's never a wonder that Disney is a leader in renowned service, as the leadership that's demonstrated by all Cast Members makes it happen.

And, as you're about to see, it takes a lot to be, as Mickey Mouse is, the "Leader of the Club."

CHAPTER FIVE

"With Great Power Comes Great Responsibility"
Leadership

In the 1998 Disney/Pixar animated film *A Bug's Life* Hopper stands before the ant colony he and other grasshoppers are terrorizing. At the moment, he is talking to the ant queen, Atta, who is attempting to deflect blame for something that happened.

Hopper leans closer to Atta and says, "First rule of leadership: *everything* is your fault."[9]

It's a dark, cynical moment, and a "bad guy" is spouting this line. But, in its ominous way, there's truth in this line of dialogue.

Before you close the book and say, "Really? Inspiration about leadership from a Disney villain?!?" hear me out.

In leadership, everything being your fault means that leadership brings responsibility for *everything* you are responsible for, be it good or not so good.

In addition to Hopper, the same has been said in various ways by many other people, from:

> "The buck stops here"
>> – President Harry S. Truman's philosophy (and a sign he kept on his desk).

To:

> "Remember, with great power comes great responsibility."
>> – Uncle Ben, in the 2002 film *Spider-Man*.

---

9 *A Bugs Life* page, IMDb.com (accessed July 25, 2023).

There are many other articles, blogs, books, and inspirational quotes about leadership, but sometimes the best way to learn about leadership is by *being* a leader.

That's how I learned.

I had never been in any other type of leadership position before working for Disney. I had always been "reporting in to" the manager, the supervisor, the "boss." Regarding responsibility, I had always been looking to someone else.

Disney changed all of that. During my second year working for the company, I was approached by several of my leaders and asked if I had ever considered being a manager, or a leader, with Disney. I kept politely declining. I was flattered but was content in my current role.

During my Disney's Animal Kingdom stint, my leader Tammy asked me to join her on a walk in an area with the Executive General Manager, Robert, who wanted some insight from us. During the walk, Robert asked me questions and sought out my opinion. All the while, as he always did, taking the time to thoughtfully listen.

Afterward, Tammy took me aside and asked, "Are you *sure* you don't want to be a leader?" After I replied no, she then added, "Well, you just showed some leadership qualities there on the walk. You should think about it."

I was struck. Leadership qualities? Me? Really? I'm the person who couldn't manage to separate white clothes from colored clothes when doing laundry!

But it made me think that if someone had that much faith in me, maybe I needed to have some faith in myself.

I spoke to Tammy shortly after this and expressed my concerns: I didn't know much about running a business as a leader. "Well, that's something you should learn more about," she said. I also said that what was really concerning was that leaders make decisions daily, and everyone looks to them for guidance. I had no experience with that.

Tammy then explained that I could get experience with that every day. I could be what she termed "a leader among my peers." Naively, I had an image of myself telling my fellow Cast Members what to do, followed by them showing me the door.

What I learned was that everyone can demonstrate leadership qualities. If I started thinking about what decisions I could make and be a peer to my peers, I could demonstrate leadership qualities and begin to get myself comfortable with all that leaders do; I could get myself comfortable with being a leader.

Best of all, Tammy said she would help me with this. And she did, becoming a mentor and preparing me for a future role as a leader. If Tammy couldn't impart information, she would guide me to others who would partner so I could continue learning.

There wasn't a light switch flipped from "Off" to "Leadership," but it was more like a dimmer switch that was being turned ever-so-slowly, and the light of leadership was beginning to illuminate my mind, as low a 40-watt bulb as that is.

With guidance from Tammy and others, I later went through a panel interview and, about a week later, received a congratulatory call that I would be promoted to Retail Guest Service Manager in an area of World Showcase at Epcot.

There's a moment in a 1973 movie entitled *The Candidate* where Robert Redford plays Bill McKay, a candidate for U.S. Senate, with little chance of winning…and then, at the end of the film, he surprises everyone when he does.

In a famous last line of the film, he turns to his team and asks, "What do we do now?"

That was my first thought when I learned I would be a leader. However, unlike Bill McKay, I was lucky to have many who had helped boost my confidence and had faith in me, which helped tremendously.

Like everything else in life, I realized leadership would be about learning *and* learning as I go. It was going to be the first day of school again. This time the first day of leadership.

And, just like Traditions and other training, Disney would ensure I had enough preparation. It was a time of building on all I knew and learning to take it in a new direction.

My first days of leadership involved several days of wearing the costume worn by the Cast in the areas where I would be leading. I would be trained as if it *was* my first day with the company and I *was* a brand-new Cast Member.

It was the perfect way to begin my leadership journey. Working those days in the merchandise shops in the Germany, Italy, and American Adventure pavilions, I'm not quite sure I cut quite the figure in my costume (especially those lederhosen!), but I was able to see and learn the area first-hand from the Cast.

Not only did I work all the different positions, but I was able to take a break with the Cast in the break room. Some of them didn't know I was a new manager in the area, so I also received an honest and open opinion about what some of the challenges in the area were (it was an actual *Undercover Boss* moment years before that show was even a thing).

When those same Cast realized I was a leader, there was a moment of wide-eyed shock, followed by an apology. I told them not to, and I appreciated the honesty. And I did; this in-costume experience was an invaluable and irreplicable way to begin my career as a leader.

The Cast Members would remember this and often mention it to me during my two years as a leader in the area. It meant much more than that *"Undercover Boss* moment." One of the Cast Members would often say they would never forget seeing me working in costume.

For the longest time, I thought it was because the sight of me in that costume was enough to elicit polite chuckles. Then, one day, the Cast Member added that they would never forget it because it meant a lot to them; they felt I cared enough about what they did that I was willing to do it myself.

From then on, whenever I transitioned to a new role or area, I would always make time for "in-costume" training.

After this training with Cast, it was time for my training as a leader alongside my peers. I would learn everything about being a leader throughout the day –how to open the area at the start of the day and close out the area when the park would close.

Much like all training at Disney, I learned this first-hand, working alongside one of my peers on the leadership team, serving as their "shadow," so to speak. I would learn from a variety and spectrum of experience: a seasoned leader who, at the time, had over two decades of experience with Disney and another who had just started about six months before I had.

Through it all, the daily responsibilities were taught to me: Safety, first and foremost, which involved not just keeping an eye out for any safety concerns, but also responding to a safety concern involving a Guest or Cast Member. This required answering calls on the radio, used for communication among all leaders throughout the park. There was also cash handling, securing the locations, and walking the shops to ensure they were fully stocked and ready for the "Show."

While these were extremely important, my peers also taught me, in practice and from their experience, how to navigate other "non-technical" aspects of a leadership day. Just as merchandise Cast were balancing ringing on the register or stocking a shelf with Guest service, leaders would need to balance their responsibilities with Cast *and* Guest service.

During training, a Cast Member asked a question about their schedule, and the leader I was shadowing said they would get back to them the next day. The leader wrote it down, making sure to let me know we needed to follow up the next day, even if we didn't have an answer yet, and were still waiting on the information.

Another day, we received a call about a Guest situation in the pavilion we had just left. The leader I was shadowing said that we needed to get back there quickly and informed me that whenever we received a call about a Guest or Cast situation, no matter what we were doing (even if it was heading in a different direction), we needed to get there.

I watched as my peer masterfully talked with a Guest who was upset at having to wait longer than they expected. The Guest had a FastPass for the then brand-new Mission: Space attraction and was afraid of missing the window of time, and my peer, partnering with the Mission: Space team with a phone call, made sure that they wouldn't.

Another Cast Member approached us about a concern. It seems they weren't seeing eye-to-eye with a fellow Cast Member, and there was some tension. The leader listened and talked the Cast Member through the situation, coming up with several ideas for a resolution.

This, and more, I had observed as part of *my* leader's day-to-day. Now, *I* was going to need to do this day-to-day.

Which I did within days. While training, my peers, whom I was shadowing, began to place the day's decisions squarely in my lap. Cast Member had a question, I was charged with finding the solution and getting back to them. Difficult Guest situation? I would talk with the Guest (and my first was a doozy involving a Guest who injured themselves). Difficult Cast Member situation? I would be the one who would be talking to the Cast Member.

This was the best leadership training possible. *Being* a leader is the best way to learn about leadership.

It was early into my leadership journey, during those initial days in World Showcase at Epcot, that I was able to attend a seminar conducted by Lee Cockerell, then the Executive Vice President, Operations at Walt Disney World.

Lee said something that became like a "true North" for me during my leadership journey. I wish I could remember the exact phrase, but the handwritten note I had on my desk for years paraphrased Lee's words from the seminar like this:

"As a leader, if you're not out there every day working on your reputation, don't worry; others will create one for you."

That meant so much to me and still does. What you do is who you are. Actions do speak louder than words.

I sometimes learned this the hard way. Just as the Cast noticed what I did, they also saw what I didn't do. And, sometimes, simply paying attention to the most minor thing could change it for the better.

Several years later, I encountered a Cast Member in a World Showcase stockroom who couldn't remember the last time we saw each other.

And, in their one comment, I knew that I had just become "The leader who never stops to talk to, or check in with, the stock Cast Members." That reputation had just been created for me. It wasn't on purpose. There was so much going on, on stage, and the stock team kept things flowing so well backstage that it became a blind spot for me. I knew that had to change, and I would need to start making time to check in with the stock team, no matter what else was going on.

It's easy for your reputation to get away from you and for you to become what you don't want to be:

The leader who doesn't follow up.
The leader who doesn't want to talk to Guests who are upset.
The leader who doesn't like to discuss challenging Cast situations.

Nevertheless, when you avoid doing these, then that's who you become…and it doesn't take long to become that "doesn't" leader…and it takes even longer to get that "doesn't" removed from your name, (some sort of surgery may be required).

Of course, you can't possess a superhero sense of self-awareness, so how do you know what you are not doing? It's through the "gift" that's often discussed. You know, the one that keeps on giving and is often returned:

Feedback.

If you can't see those "blind spots," then there are times when you need to ask others about them. Sometimes feedback is freely given, and sometimes it's not. Most people aren't comfortable giving feedback.

There's a joke in the Woody Allen film *Annie Hall* (I know, I know, not Disney, but stick with me on this) that goes like this:

"…this guy goes to a psychiatrist and says, 'Doc, uh, my brother's crazy; he thinks he's a chicken.' And, uh, the doctor says, 'Well, why don't you turn him in?' The guy says, 'Well, I would, but I need the eggs.'"[10]

In the movie, this as an analogy for love, but this could also be a correlation for why most people don't provide feedback to others. Most people know there's an issue, which may even bother them, but they don't want to "make waves" or "cause drama." They will just "live with it." They don't want to turn in their brother, who thinks he's a chicken, because they feel they "need the eggs."

There may be times that *you* have to *ask* for feedback; you can't wait for it. I learned that's part of being a leader. Martin, one of the the Magic Kingdom leaders I worked with, used to end every meeting with his direct reports, peers, partners, and leader by saying, "What am I not doing for you that I could be doing for you?"

It was a perfect way to elicit feedback more subtly and without using the word "feedback." Sometimes, just saying

---

10 *Annie Hall* page, IMDb.com (accessed June 5, 2023).

"feedback" is like actual feedback from a microphone blaring from a speaker. No one wants to hear it. But it needs to be discussed, especially if it is "constructive feedback" (the very positive way of saying, "You're doing something wrong, and I'd like you to start doing it right").

And when you receive this type of feedback, it is illuminating and can change your way of thinking and your actions for the better.

When I was a Magic Kingdom Merchandise Training Manager, my leader asked me to solicit feedback from the merchandise leaders I was supporting. So, as I met with them, I asked. All seemed to be going great, so I placed it on my agenda for a meeting. And, as I asked the first leader I met with, I received feedback...*very blunt* constructive feedback.

"What?!?" I thought. "Things are great! Shouldn't it all be 'positive feedback,' after which I am victoriously carried through the hallway on everyone's shoulders?"

Nope. I received a healthy dose of constructive feedback. Things had been going well, but these were my "blind spots." Things I wasn't even aware of needed improvement, but they did.

And that was something else that I learned; as a leader, if you are going to ask for feedback, be ready to receive it. More importantly, be prepared to act upon it and follow up with those who provided it.

I knew, at that moment, upon receiving the feedback I wasn't expecting, that's exactly what I had to do, and I did. Doing so was followed by more feedback, but happily, this time, it was positive.

Giving feedback is another leadership skill that can be developed. One of the major elements of giving feedback is promptness.

If I were to say, "Remember that thing that you did that time on that one Friday in March a few years ago? Well, you did it terribly," it doesn't help at all, and now you feel rotten.

Feedback, positive or constructive, must be given as soon as possible. One year in early January, after a hectic holiday season at Epcot, during which our team broke several different records, our leader Angie brought a bottle of sparkling cider and appetizers to our staff meeting to thank us all for the previous weeks.

If she had waited just a few more weeks, we still would've been appreciative (even with non-alcoholic champagne), but it wouldn't have resonated with us all the same way as time had passed and we were beginning to move on. Her positive feedback was perfect in its timeliness.

And, if the feedback is constructive, timeliness is critical to make corrections. If the person you deliver the feedback to says, "Why didn't you tell me sooner?" it's most likely too late.

Also, there's a big difference between "You could be doing better" and "Here's *how* you could be doing better."

Constructive feedback should also be accompanied by coaching, teaching, input, and ideas on how the individual could be more effective.

I once had a leader who reported to me who was struggling to meet deadlines. When we met and I provided feedback, it became clear that a feeling of being overwhelmed was making things spin out of control.

We discussed time management, and I discussed what worked best for me and provided resources. After this, I committed to having a weekly meeting, specifically to discuss time management and find out how the organizational journey was progressing. Slowly but surely, the leader began to feel more in control and met deadlines.

It would have been easy to provide feedback and let the leader take it from there. But, honestly, how can you say, "You really need to work on your time management. Now…make time…to do that."

So many avoid constructive feedback. "I'm just not good with conflict" seems to have become a mantra. Don't worry; you're not alone. Few go to work, rubbing their hands and saying, "All right! Bring on this awkward, uncomfortable moment!"

That said, it needs to be dealt with, and it's part of a leader's job. If the "not comfortable with" mantra is something you find yourself saying over and over, find someone who has experience with feedback and ask for advice, and input.

You may never be comfortable with providing this feedback—few people are. But the more you learn how to provide it correctly, you will learn to provide it empathetically. And your feedback will be more meaningful.

Additionally, when delivering constructive feedback, it's also essential that the individual understand the feedback that's being given. I learned that everyone receives feedback differently, but however it's delivered, the message *must* get across.

Sometimes this involves re-stating the feedback differently to ensure the message is received. I facilitated a class at Disney that used a scene from Walt Disney's classic 1967 animated feature, *The Jungle Book*, to illustrate how to re-state feedback until it's finally clearly delivered.

The sequence shown was a conversation between Baloo the bear and Bagheera the panther. Bagheera wants to get the young boy Mowgli (the "man cub") back to the "man-village." Bagheera knows Mowgli won't survive in the jungle with the villain Shere Kahn, the tiger.

Baloo doesn't understand why Mowgli must return with the other humans and wants him to stay in the jungle. Bagheera attempts to explain it to Baloo, but the bear continues to be flippant. He isn't "getting it." Finally, Bagheera cuts to the chase:

"Bagheera: [getting irritated] Baloo, you've got to be serious...

Baloo: Oh, stop worrying, Baggy! Stop worrying! I'll take care of him.

Bagheera: Yes, like you did when the monkeys kidnapped him, huh?

Baloo: Can't a guy make one mistake?

Bagheera: Not in the jungle! And another thing, sooner or later, Mowgli will meet Shere Khan.

Baloo: The tiger? What's he got against the kid?

Bagheera: He hates man with a vengeance. You know that! Because he fears man's gun and man's fire.

Baloo: But little Mowgli don't have those things.

Bagheera: Shere Khan won't wait until he does. He'll get Mowgli while he's young and helpless. Just one swipe!

Baloo: Oh! Well, what...what are we going to do?

Bagheera: Do what's best for the boy.

Baloo: You better believe it! You name it; I'll do it.

Bagheera: Good. Then make Mowgli go to the man-village."[11]

---

11 *The Jungle Book* (1967) page, IMDb.com (accessed November 1, 2022).

A seemingly simple dialogue exchange from *The Jungle Book* provides a lot of insight into ensuring that feedback is received. Bagheera must state and re-state his thoughts several times and in several different ways until Baloo finally understands that it's a life-and-death situation, and that's why he needs to get Mowgli to the man-village.

Feedback like this comprises a large part of what a leader does, but within it and, in fact, within *everything* a leader does, there's something else—inspiration.

While this may seem like a very ethereal part of the role of leadership, the concept of motivating others can indeed be discussed, imparted, or taught in a classroom. However, when inspiration happens, it is something that grows out of relationships and moments.

There's an apt quote from Shakespeare's play Twelfth Night (if you had that in your Bingo card for "things you never thought you'd read in this book," you win):: "Some are born great, some achieve greatness, and others have greatness thrust upon them."[12]

When it comes to inspiration and leadership, it seems that those who are great at it have it "thrust upon them."

Leaders are called upon to inspire others in "larger" and "smaller" moments in good times and bad. I saw this and experienced this several times while I was with Disney.

Inspirational leadership does involve saying those inspiring words at a presentation or a meeting that stays with you.

"Don't dwell on today. Live in today."

"The next generation of leadership is looking to us."

"They say on your deathbed, you'll never wish you spent more time at the office. But I will. Gotta be a lot better than a deathbed." (Borrowed from the TV show, *The Office*). [13]

"So oftentimes it happens that we live our lives in chains. And we never even know we have the key." (Borrowed from The Eagles' song, "I'm Already Gone"). [14]

All of these are quotes from, and utilized by, leaders I worked with at Disney. They still stay with me. As do many of

---

12 Brainyquote.com (accessed August 21, 2023).
13 Quotes.net (accessed June 8, 2023).
14 Genius.com (accessed June 8, 2023).

Walt Disney's quotes. My favorite—"You can design and create and build the most wonderful place in the world. But it takes people to make the dream a reality."[15]

Just as, if not more, inspirational are the actions that leaders take.

While working as a Magic Kingdom Merchandise Training Manager, I was having lunch with a peer, Scott, when we were approached by one of the park's Executive General Managers, Dan. He asked if he could join us for lunch. We said sure.

Throughout our time together, we didn't talk about work—we discussed our families, movies, and sports—it was nice. After, Scott and I, somewhat star-struck, told our team that one of the executives had joined us for lunch, we found out that this was something Dan did on a regular basis.

Instead of having lunch with his peers or grabbing a sandwich in his office, Dan would have lunch in the cafeteria, sit with the Cast and get to know them.

Inspiring. It inspired me to do the same. For the next thirteen years I was with Disney; I would make time to take my lunch in a nearby break room or cafeteria and talk with Cast.

Years later, while at the Airport shops, we had a retirement party for one of the Cast Members. On the same day, one of my former leaders, Mike, was also retiring from Disney after 40 years. As we were serving food and cutting cake, while making speeches and reminiscing in the break room, who walked through the door, but Mike.

On *his* last day, *his* retirement day, Mike drove from Walt Disney World property to Orlando International Airport to attend the retirement party for a Cast Member. The latter didn't even report to him anymore. The Cast Member was thrilled. We all were.

Inspiring. Again, it inspired me to do the same. From that day on, I cleared my calendar whenever there was a celebration for a Cast Member, one I currently worked with or had worked with in the past.

"Cast first. Guest always. Everything else follows." Beverly, one of the General Managers I worked with, would say this as

---

15 Brainyquote.com (accessed June 8, 2023).

a mantra. It's too true, and has stayed with *me* as a mantra, as that is what leadership is all about.

Being a leader with Disney was like getting an education *and* a degree in leadership every day.

Leadership is about being there for those you lead, building relationships, and caring for them. At Disney, this was done from the earliest days as a leader, through in-costume training (walking in their shoes), following up on requests, developing Cast, recognizing Cast, and, just as Disney does for Guests, making Cast feel special.

When I transitioned to a role as a "leader of leaders," the same applied, and my role was also about developing leaders and supporting them to become better in their roles. I learned that it's knowing when to step in and to set up the leader for success, just as Tammy had set me up for success as I was on my leadership journey.

A leader once offered the opinion that they thought that good leadership was about delegation. I disagreed—it can't *all* be about delegation. You need to provide leaders with all they need to succeed, not just hand it off to them.

As a leader, you learn from other leaders—what to do and what *not* to do. From there, you take what you want from the "leadership buffet," adopting the attributes of those leaders you admire, putting them on your plate, and mixing in a lot of yourself, to create your leadership style.

As Hopper in *A Bug's Life* had said, in leadership, everything *may* be your fault, but it's really your responsibility, and as Beverly said, "Cast first, Guest always, and everything else follows."

But what about that "everything else?" As a leader, how do you keep up with meeting financial requirements, your budget, and adjusting labor and staffing as needed?

You think, as a leader, a lot of the business is none of your business? Think again.

CHAPTER SIX

More Than a Numbers Game
Business

Bandleader Lawrence Welk once told the cast of his popular TV show, "Look like you're having fun, but don't have any."[16]

If you don't know who Lawrence Welk is, ask your parents... better yet, ask your grandparents...or head over to Wikipedia. The important thing is his quote and advice. Welk was essentially telling the dancers, singers, and musicians on his show that they needed to put hard work into the entertainment that they were providing to the audience at home. The audience shouldn't see any of the hard work, just the entertainment; they should all "look like they're having fun."

In many ways, this is true at Walt Disney World. Guests arrive at the parks, resorts, and water parks each day, completely immersed in the Disney magic they were looking for, unaware of the hard work behind it. And that's the way it should be.

When you go food shopping and buy milk, you are blissfully unaware that the right amount of milk must be ordered, the delivery has to be scheduled, employees have to be staffed to stock the freezer, and a process has to be put in place to keep it fresh. If you think of all that every time you carry your milk to the register, you are either employed by a supermarket or a profound thinker. Usually, you're just buying milk and then moving on with your life.

But the fact is, there is a tremendous amount of business behind what it took to get that milk to the shelf. And there's also a tremendous amount of business behind bringing Disney magic to Guests.

---

16 Laughbreak.com (accessed July 20, 2023).

A Cast Member learns the effort behind the "Show" from day one. This is another part of Traditions class—learning to balance Cast, Guest, and Business Results.

To illustrate, here are some extreme examples, seemingly right out of a Disney fairy tale:

If all the Cast were allowed to have summers off, there would be a lot of happy Cast Members, but Guests who look forward to their Walt Disney World summer vacations would be bummed (to say the least) by the fact that the Resort would be closed June through August. Conversely, the quarterly earnings report wouldn't be stellar for the period that included the summer months, and business would suffer.

Or, how's this for another "what if?":

Going back to those summer months, imagine if Disney announced that every Guest visiting would get into the Disney Parks for free (stop laughing, this is my example). What a unique, magical Guest experience that would be. However, what would the experience be for all the other Guests, not to mention Cast Members, if the Parks had unlimited free admission? The Cast experience would suffer. And all the park ticket sales from that summer that the company would have used to re-invest in new attractions, resorts, and other expansions wouldn't be there. Business wouldn't be looking too good.

Neither example, both wildly exaggerated, makes good business sense, or a good Guest experience.

And now, back to reality:

Ensuring that Cast is supported by leadership and has the resources they need for their jobs will allow them to provide an experience that exceeds Guest expectations. Those Guests will become recurring Guests, which will positively impact the Business.

In Traditions class, an example of the legs of a stool is used to illustrate this. If Cast, Guest, and Business aren't all in synch, if all the "legs" aren't equal, the stool won't balance.

As a leader, a large part of your role is creating that balance. If you are focused on just Cast or Guest (or both), the Business Results will suffer, and everything will be out of balance.

Honestly, when I came to work for the Walt Disney World Resort, I wanted to be a part of those significant Guest situations I had seen and been a part of when I visited, and I wanted to work with my fellow Cast Members to create memories.

What I didn't want to do was read financial spreadsheets that provided information on how the merchandise shops were doing or review labor and staffing levels to see if they were appropriate.

This is going to sound incredibly irresponsible, but to be honest...it just seemed like there was a lot of math there, and I had never been good at math. I love that Meme that circulates now and then: "Well, another day has passed, and I still haven't used algebra."

Ten-year-old me vowed that when I got out of school, I would try to use math as little as possible. Unfortunately, adult me tried to live up to this, and I now apologize to all my math teachers whose lives I made a living hell.

It's no revelation to say that math is necessary in our lives. For many of us who struggled with math in school, we look back and realize that it's one of the parts of our lives that was, and is, necessary to make it well-rounded.

The same is true as we get older; there are aspects of our lives that we may not feel competent in, but we need them, we need to learn more about them, and we need to know how we get ourselves more comfortable with them, to make ourselves more well-rounded.

I wish I had read the above paragraph when I first became a leader. Feeling very comfortable with the Cast and Guest aspects, I figured I would do the only logical thing: ignore the Business side. After all, that wasn't really "my thing," and it will probably take care of itself, right?

I couldn't have been more wrong. Fortunately, I learned this early in my leadership career and was very upfront with my leader, at the time, about it.

One afternoon, I was walking through the Heritage Manor shop at the American Adventure pavilion with my leader, Jim. We walked over to some new merchandise we had just received in the shop. These were action figures of great leaders in American history: George Washington, Abraham Lincoln, and Benjamin Franklin. They were cool.

Jim asked me how the action figures were doing. "Oh, no," I thought. "It's a business question."

I managed the most intelligent answer I could muster: "Yeah...ya know...pretty good."

Jim then asked what sales were like and if there was one that was selling better than the others.

I wanted to point and say, "Well, George Washington, obviously, he *was* the first President." But, like George himself, I couldn't tell a lie, and after a minute, I admitted to Jim that I didn't know.

Jim knew I didn't know, but he was also a great leader and willing to help me. After that walk, I talked with Jim about the Business Results side of things and how it wasn't my "forte."

While that may be the case, he talked to me about it being part of my job, and I needed to find a way to *make it* my "forte" and find "a way in" to make myself comfortable with it.

Up to that point, when I received reports on how the shops were performing e-mailed to me from the Finance team, I would save them to a "look at later" file. When the performances of the shops would be discussed, I would fight for my eyes not to glaze over.

Jim taught me to become more comfortable with those "oh-so intimidating" spreadsheets and how to read them. He also partnered me with a peer on my team, Neil, who was very good at discussing business. As we began to meet regularly, what seemed so unfamiliar suddenly began to feel just a little more familiar. Where were these guys when I slogged through junior high math class?

Jim also connected me with partners. This was an invaluable lesson: when it came to the business, I wasn't in this alone, and it wasn't all on me. There were other teams filled with subject matter experts who could help me be successful. As with so much at Disney, it was all about being a team.

At Disney merchandise, two partnering departments were at the top of the list: Location Planning (now Location Strategy) and Visual (now Merchandise Presentation). These two teams took care of the "art and science" of merchandise, and they both did it while supporting the area's story and theme.

A walk of a shop and a meeting with members of the Visual team (the art side of merchandise) could begin a dialogue around simply changing how the product is displayed or even how introducing signs could make a difference in bringing it to Guests' attention and subsequently positively impact sales.

This thinking has been used for years in many retail organizations, particularly at Disney. For any of us who had shopped at the Disney Store when they were at our local malls, we may remember that they had something they called "plush mountain." While this may sound like an entertaining attraction, it was a mountain of plush (stuffed Disney characters) on a stairstep-like fixture in the back of the shop. "Plush mountain" was usually under a screen showing the latest Disney video that had been released.

With this placement, the Disney Store knew how much children love plush and stuffed animals. So, they knew if children could see the very top of "plush mountain" from the front of the store as they entered, it would bring them further into the store. This continues to be the Walt Disney World process, as well. The Visual team makes the product presentation aesthetically inviting to ensure the Guests make their way through the store and over to the product.

Once the Guest gets to the product, the Visual team adds details, such as signage, props, or clothing, presented on a mannequin to highlight the presentation. When I was at World of Disney, *Cars 3* was released. As the product for the film was set in the shop, the Visual team placed it not on tables but on large canisters reproducing oil barrels (complete with the "Dinoco" logo from the film on the side). It made for a highly appealing presentation and helped support the story.

In addition to these "larger picture" ideas, the Visual team also gets into such smaller details as which piece of clothing looks the best hanging and which looks best folded.

This Visual team is also responsible for designing the windows outside some shops or even creating the shops' entryways to entice Guests to enter. And this is also the team that will work closely with the team of Imagineers to ensure that a consistent story is being told in an area.

I learned they were the first of several invaluable partners by meeting with and walking the shops with the Visual team. They could help grow the business with their creative skills that could spot better aesthetic placement of product or the addition of signage.

Jim also directed me to the team that handled the "science" side of merchandise: Location Planning. This team applies a strategy for what product is carried in which shop and the "why" behind that.

For example, certain shops may be "destinations" for specific products (one shop might offer just headwear, another might sell consumables or snacks). Larger shops, such as World of Disney or Emporium, will have specific sections organized this way.

This allows for an appropriate selection of products for Guests at a specific park or resort and allows inventory to be equalized and for product sales to be tracked.

The Location Planning team looks to balance inventory between a park or between parks and resorts (ex: if stock is abundant, it will be spread out, or if it is too little, it will be consolidated).

Product may be carried in a shop, because it compliments other items offered (as an example, some *Star Wars* product may be placed in Tomorrowland in the Magic Kingdom, as it makes sense).

Just as supermarkets place staples like milk and eggs near the back of the store, this team will also place product in a shop location in the back of a park to drive traffic there and place products adjacent to other products to complement that (ex: hats and t-shirts).

Have you ever entered a bustling Walt Disney World shop during the holidays, walked right into a display of Christmas product, stopped to look at it, and noticed most others stopping to look, too? That is part of what Location Planning does—they strategically place specific products in the shop based on Guest traffic. Using technology, the Planning team can see which shop door is most active and identify the most popular or highly sought-after product to be placed there.

The team also looks at the product's sales performance and the history of the product's performance over time. Based on this, inventory would then be expanded or reduced, working closely with the operation's stock team.

I learned all of this while walking the shops with the Location Planning team; I never looked at the shops the same way again. There was a newfound realization of why the product was where it was and how that placement could make a tremendous difference when it came to business.

Both the Visual and Location Planning teams taught me that I didn't have to have all the answers when it came to business; they became great support in knowing where to go to ask the questions and get the answers.

So did the Finance team. Let me tell you, as a "math-phobic" (new word, just coined it), walking into the office of the Finance Manager was intimidating; this person knew more about numbers than the number of math problems I got incorrect in seventh grade.

But, again, Jim discussed how they were another valued partner. Finance would make projections on budgets for different lines of businesses at Walt Disney World based on forecasts for attendance at the parks and occupancy at the resorts.

Meeting with the Finance manager was significant for that reason alone—I mean, if you are trying to make money with your business, it's good to know, ya know, *how much* money you're supposed to make.

Taking a closer look at revenue also allowed the Finance team to determine, early on, where there were opportunities for revenue (in other words, where money isn't being made) and where too much money is being spent—multiple times in my two decades with Disney, a "heads up" from Finance, led to a discovery that *way* too much was being spent on re-ordering supplies that we already had in abundance.

The Finance team also provided insight into the cost of your Labor (or staffing), which could lead to conversations about how best to utilize your Labor…

…which led to connecting with another critical partner: the Labor Manager and Scheduler. Meeting with this team shed light on how Cast Members were scheduled for their various shifts, as well as why schedules were created (here's an illuminating thought: busier times of the day, month, or year required more people to be scheduled at that time. I know, I know, your mind is now blown).

I also learned that generating a schedule is like putting together a complex jigsaw puzzle where all the pieces must fit correctly if the business is to run effectively.

As I would come back to the area, after meeting with these teams, armed and educated with new information, I would think about what I had learned. There's so much in a day at Disney that leaders have no control over, and those "uncontrollables" can impact the business.

First and foremost is the weather. Disney has yet to introduce the mythical "dome," which has been discussed as an urban legend for years. As a regular Disney Guest, you may have heard the jokes about raising the dome over a park when the regularly scheduled thunderstorm arrives.

If only. Maybe someday, after the statewide air conditioning is installed in Florida. For now, it's the stuff of Disney fantasy, and when that afternoon deluge hits and Guests swarm into your shop, you have no control over that and how it may impact running the business.

As a leader, I myself couldn't control attendance at Disney. There are projections, but during busier seasons, attendance would exceed those projections. It's not possible to just stand out in front of the theme park as a traffic cop, only letting in the number of Guests that your shop could assist.

My position gave me no control over the price of a product. There was a team at Disney that set those prices based on various factors. And, you had no control over what product was available in your shop. The Planning team would make this determination based on the theme and story of your shop (*Star Wars* light sabers may be the hottest thing but would look severely out of place in Tinker Bell's Treasures), as well as inventory availability and other factors.

Leaders may influence their product if they receive enough Guest requests and data and then provide that feedback to the correct sources.

So, what the heck do leaders have, at least some, control over, or what can they influence?

Leaders could influence the metrics of their business.

MORE THAN A NUMBERS GAME

Metrics?!? That sounds like more math, but don't turn to the next chapter and search for more stories of pixie dust. There is some exciting pixie dust here, just that of another kind.

Metrics are a part of leading a business, in this case, merchandise, and as I learned how to best influence them, it became a new kind of magic.

Among these metrics that became part of our everyday language were:

- The budget, which estimated what the shop might make in revenue in a given day.
- Labor goals: labor hours we were budgeted for the day.
- Units per transaction: how many items were purchased in each transaction.
- Average dollar sale: amount spent in each transaction.
- The number of transactions themselves.
- Conversion, which is used in many major retail organizations. Some stores have devices by the door that count how much Guest traffic is coming into the shop and then look at that traffic compared to the transactions. Leaders can see how many Guests are being converted to a sale (hence, conversion). This is something that a leader can influence by ensuring that Cast Members provide excellent guest service and are available for the Guests and connecting them with those tangible memories.

Hold on, I know; your eyes might be blurring. You're thinking, I bought a book to learn about Disney pixie dust, not receive a bullet-pointed list from my college elective class "Retail 101." But what I learned was that there is pixie dust that can be applied to these metrics.

Even though these are "numbers" and seem very static, they are something a leader can influence and gain control of.

I learned by employing the creative Guest Engagement by Cast Members that Disney is so well-known for; just as Mickey (at the Airport) said, "Every Guest has a story. Our job is to find out what that story is."

A leader I worked with once commented that they felt that Cast engaging Guests would *always* positively impact business results. I disagreed with the definitive nature of that. So many other factors (such as the "uncontrollables" mentioned above) come into play that it's not always a guarantee…but it's *definitely* a step in the right direction.

I learned how labor is utilized is the first line of defense and a most powerful tool in creating a successful business. We had a lot of conversations about how to best utilize staffing. Labor goals are usually established by Finance and Workload teams. You might not be able to increase or decrease your labor, but how are Cast positioned in the shop to best meet Guest needs?

I saw this first-hand while managing the shop, Image Works, which was at the exit of the Journey Into Imagination attraction. As it served as the exit, Guests would usually walk briskly through the shop, as if it was just a hallway filled with merchandise, and they would head right out the exit.

The leadership team tried something: we strategically placed Cast right in the path of the Guests, and they would greet and interact with Guests as they were leaving. Sometimes, Cast would be holding or demonstrating certain products. We found that this slowed the Guest flow; they realized that there was a merchandise shop around them, and business improved.

Cast and Guest interaction was the major piece that we could control when it came to the business, and this realization allowed me to learn about the metrics of the business and how to best influence them.

There would also be times when special merchandise was offered on a specific day during an event. Guests would queue ahead, waiting to get into the shop to browse the merchandise. Many teams found that if Cast Members could be available to walk the line and hand out merchandise "menus" to the Guests in line, it made for a much better and more efficient experience and assisted the business.

The" menus" would have pictures, descriptions, and prices of the product, allowing the Guests to decide what they wanted while in line so that they were prepared when they went in, and may have even spotted something they didn't realize was available.

This was a way to "steer" your "controllables" away from any potential "icebergs" (hey, *Titanic* is a 20th Century-Fox film, so that sort of counts as another Disney reference!).

Throughout the day at Walt Disney World merchandise shops, we could review and utilize the daily metrics to see how they can influence the business.

Being the "math whiz" (again, feel free to insert a sarcastic tone here) that I was, I carried the numbers I needed around with me on a piece of paper (later, I e-mailed them to myself each day. How technologically advanced of me...again, sarcasm).

This was a way for me to "relate" to the numbers, as I would walk the operation and see how I could influence them.

"Oh, come on," you're saying (yes, I can hear you). "Guests at Walt Disney World have so much on their minds and so much to do in a day; just having a Cast Member talk with them isn't going to help business. And, Cast Members never act like "used car salespeople" (Try these Mickey slippers on and take them for a spin around the block) Trying to sell, sell, sell comes across as just a numbers game."

It's much more than just a numbers game.

Consider this example: A Cast Member is positioned by the front door of a shop, greeting Guests as they enter. In addition to creating a great first impression, as they say, "Hi," they also notice a Guest who is wearing a T-shirt with Marvel comics characters on it.

The Cast Member comments on how much they like the shirt and mentions that there are shirts available featuring the latest Marvel film. The Guest was unaware of this and goes to the display and picks out a shirt. A Cast Member nearby mentions that the same characters are featured on a coffee mug and walks them over. The Guest decides to purchase the mug, as well.

The Guest then heads over to the register to check out, and by positioning staffing in just the right spot, the business has been positively influenced.

The Guest, who was unaware of the Marvel product and may have just been "passing through," made a purchase (conversion has been influenced); they purchased two items (average dollar sale and units per transaction have been influenced). And, because they bought the product, transactions have been influenced, which in turn could assist with meeting or exceeding budget.

And it was all done by creating the positive, easy, stress-free experience that Guests want from Disney. I saw the above example happen many times in so many different locations.

While at the Once Upon a Toy shop, during the summer of 2013, we were slated to feature merchandise from the Disney/Pixar feature, *Monsters University*. As good luck would have it, a contact from the Marketing team let me know that they had "life size" statues of Mike and Sully that we could use in the shop for the opening weekend of the movie, and it could make for a great "photo-op" for Guests.

Partnering with the Visual and Location Strategy team, we were able to have the Mike and Sully statues positioned right near the *Monsters University* product. When Guests came into the shop, one of the first things they saw were the Monsters, right next to all the new products.

And there was also a Cast Member there to greet them, offer to take their picture and another Cast Member available to discuss all of the new *Monsters University* merchandise.

The Cast loved doing this, the Guests had a great, unique experience, and Business was very good that weekend.

But, what if Once Upon a Toy didn't have the statues of Mike and Sully? What if we didn't receive any of the product from the film? Those would have been two of the "uncontrollables" that we could face. And, if that was the case, we would look to what we *could* control—allowing the Cast to create a different experience and discuss what product *was* available.

As the Rolling Stones sang, "You Can't Always Get What You Want" (I am claiming the first Rolling Stones reference in a Disney-related book). This would sometimes be true about the merchandise that you would carry.

One other time at Once Upon a Toy, just before the holiday season was to begin, we began carrying the very popular Walt Disney World Christmas railroad toy train. Just before Thanksgiving, we received word that we were to transfer all our inventory of the toy trains to World of Disney.

As you can imagine, this didn't sit well with many of us at Once Upon a Toy, as we immediately saw World of Disney usurping all our sales. Tension began to mount at the same rate as the songs playing on the local, 24-hour Christmas music radio station.

I thought to myself that there had to be a logical explanation to his, so I reached out to our partner in Location Strategy, Lenny. He provided all the clarity I needed. Apparently, there was a new design of the Christmas train debuting soon and, to be able to place that on the sales floor, the previous version had to "sell through," and it would sell quicker at World of Disney. Once it did, both shops would get the new train.

It made perfect sense. As a team, we immediately understood that we could pivot to what was controllable. It was a learning around how a phone call, or e-mail can lead to clarity, and then can lead to what you can control.

Great Guest experience from Cast *can* lead to significant business results. It's all about balancing those "legs of the stool," as we had learned in Traditions class.

These were exactly the lessons that I learned. The biggest one seemed like a no-brainer, but it was around seeking out what you don't know and always learning. There may be aspects of your job that you don't like, but you can't ignore them; they will always be there. As much as I didn't want to look over the reports on shop performance, there would be another in my e-mail inbox the following week.

I had to find a way to learn more about this in my own way. It was my job. If I didn't, things were going to get more complex.

Where to start? Look to others who can help. I was lucky to have leaders, peers, and partners who were teachers and understanding teachers, at that. It helped me to know I wasn't alone.

Thanks to them, business, which seemed like speaking another language before I started working for Disney, was a language that, with a degree of diligence, developed into something that I was fortunate enough to become proficient in.

The time that others took with me was so invaluable. We all need each other, and others rely on us.

Added to the new language I was learning was another word: mentor.

CHAPTER SEVEN

Jiminy and Obi-Wan Were Right
Mentoring

Not long after I started with the company, after a bustling night on Main Street, U.S.A., I sat in the back office of Exposition Hall, printing out the closing paperwork with one of my leaders. After finishing, he said to me, "What do you want to do with the company?"

I didn't know how to answer. I didn't know what he meant. I was doing what I wanted to do with the company; I was *working* for Disney. But it was then that I realized he was looking to learn more about me and, potentially, help me in my career.

The Walt Disney World Resort is a big place. When I was working there, there were over 70,000 Cast Members employed. That's a lot of jobs and a lot of opportunities. As a Cast Member, when you begin to think about "what you want to do with the company," as my leader had said, it can be overwhelming.

Every job looks interesting. Perhaps a role project managing upcoming events or additions to a park? Sure! Maybe designing merchandise? Yeah! What about creating new attractions? Yes!

But, then you begin to think—what am I best suited for? What do I have experience in? What am I most passionate about?

And, on top of that, how do I even find out what to do next and what my future path is? And, when I do, how do I navigate getting there?

You can easily feel like *Alice in Wonderland*, falling into the rabbit hole, where you keep falling, and falling, endlessly.

Who can help stop this "Curiouser and Curiouser" madness? A mentor.

Wait! What? A mentor, you're saying to yourself (and don't say it too loud, the other people in Starbucks are likely to stare), "Do you mean like Jiminy Cricket and Obi-Wan Kenobi?"

Yeah, pretty much. "Always let your conscience be your guide," Jiminy sang.[17] "Who is more foolish? The fool or the fool who follows him?" said Obi-Wan.[18] These are just two pieces of fantastic advice, and ya know what? Jiminy and Obi-Wan were right.

I've learned that we all need a Jiminy or an Obi-Wan. There's a reason for all this. Heroes in movies have someone that they rely on for guidance. Art imitates life.

And while our mentors may not be singing crickets or Jedi Knights, they still provide the same source of inspiration and enlightenment.

But what is a mentor anyway?

While a character of the same name inspired the word "mentor," in Homer's *Odyssey* (another nugget to drop at the next cocktail party), the *Merriam-Webster Dictionary* defines it as "a trusted counselor or guide."[19]

Great, so if you're not in Ancient Greece, how do you get a mentor?

My good friend, Christopher, who had once been a leader with Disney, as well as a Walt Disney World Ambassador, has a philosophy about mentorship: "Don't ask someone to be your mentor; tell them they're already your mentor and explain what you've learned from them and what you hope to learn from them in the future! (In other words, don't give a potential mentor the option to say 'No!')."

This perfectly sums up how to initially connect with a mentor. When I saw he posted this on social media, I immediately asked Christopher if I could share it, as this is how every mentoring relationship has happened with me.

There's no dramatic music, followed by a glowing light as you declare: "You! Yes, you! I choose you as my mentor!" While that would be cool, it's just not as formal a process as that.

---

17 Genius.com (accessed November 1, 2022).
18 *Star Wars: Episode IV—A New Hope* page, IMDb.com (accessed November 1, 2022).
19 www.merriam-webster.com.

Mentoring relationships begin through conversations and long-lasting connections. I had mentioned Tammy in the Leadership chapter and how much she guided me initially. After I transitioned to leadership, we never lost touch, and I would call on her, from time to time, to ask a question, get guidance, or even receive feedback.

All of the leaders at Disney that I would consider mentors followed in this same "mold." They would be leaders I had worked with in some capacity, and the relationship as a mentor grew naturally.

A mentor should be someone you respect; someone you want to emulate. When I first came to Epcot as a leader, Tammy told me that her husband Dru worked there and that I should reach out to him.

At the time, Dru was the manager of Mouse Gear, at Epcot, then the big, Emporium-like shop in an area of the park then known as Future World. After our meeting, Dru asked if I wanted a tour of Mouse Gear and, as he walked me through the massive shop, both on stage and backstage, I was amazed—Dru knew every Cast Member by name, would ask them about their personal lives and how they were doing and even seemed to have an in-joke with each one.

Additionally, running on a parallel track with this, Dru knew everything going on in the operation, discussing the different products and the Guest traffic flow in the business. I was striving and struggling to do this as a leader myself.

As a new leader, I had trouble verbalizing what I had for lunch that day.

After that day, I continued to stay in contact, meet, and have lunch with Dru from time to time, and he became another mentor for me.

I also learned that a mentor should provide an objective voice, someone who is outside of your current situation and, as such, can provide valuable insight.

At one point, as a leader, I was struggling. Yes, sometimes things aren't "practically perfect in every way." Something just felt "off track" at work; I was attempting to figure out what was "next" for me in my career, and as can often happen, I just felt "stuck."

I met with Jim, my former manager. As Jim wasn't close to my situation, he could evaluate it and provide an objective "outsider's" perspective.

Just thirty minutes with him, providing me with options and a different way of thinking, suddenly made me feel "unstuck." I left his office that day with hope, thanks to the advice he provided.

A mentor should also be able to provide this sound advice, (which you can keep at the forefront of your mind and then apply). While preparing for an interview as Area Manager, I met with Martin, an Area Manager himself at the Magic Kingdom. Martin had been with the company since Walt Disney World opened and had tremendous experience to draw from.

So, I asked Martin, as I prepped for the interview, that well-worn question: "What would make me stand out from the other candidates?" Martin thought about it and then began to tell me a story of one of the NBA Drafts.

"Oh," I thought, "A sports story." And my mind began to fog over. However, as Martin told the story, the fog lifted.

He told me about a college student who left school before graduation to participate in the NBA Draft. He was a highly thought-of and talented player, but he wasn't the first or second pick. He was the third.

With that third number, expectations were somewhat lower, but during his debut with the Chicago Bulls, he scored sixteen points in one game. [20]

The player, revealed Martin, was Michael Jordan.

Even though he was picked third, he showed everyone, in fact, the entire world, through his skills, dedication, and hard work, that he should've been the first pick. "That's how you stand out," said Martin.

I suddenly realized that more than anything, my work, my actions, my work ethic, and what I would do, would be most important. Unlike Michael Jordan, I couldn't dunk without a ladder, but I could do my job to the best of my abilities.

So impactful is that story that it still stays with me to this day. So much so that I've included it here.

---

20 Michael Jordan page, Wikipedia.com (accessed November 1, 2022).

Additionally, mentors should be willing to, and always have, time for you. All the leaders I met with in this capacity, no matter how busy they were or how much their calendar was full of "back-to-backs," would always meet up.

And this was important, as they always provided open, honest information and feedback—another vital attribute as a mentor. One such mentor, Mike, was also my leader at one point.

While he was my leader, we had just finished a round of leadership panel interviews, where the candidates would move on to the "next step," which would be to be placed in a "talent pool" and would, in the words of Dory, "just keep swimming," until they were chosen for a leadership role.

Getting the news that you were "moving on to the pool" was a big deal. Mike had asked me to set up a time with each candidate. However, it was a hectic week, so I came up with what I considered a more efficient plan of contacting the candidates, while still trying to keep it a personal, impactful connection.

I would *call* all of the candidates.

So off I went, right down the list, calling each of the leadership candidates and giving them the great news. I could sense their enthusiasm spilling over the phone. After I reached the last candidate and swore I heard their voice crack with emotion on the other end of the phone, I crossed the last name on the list off with a flourish.

I then sent Mike an e-mail, letting him know that all the candidates had been informed and proudly went home for the weekend.

When I returned, Mike came over to my office. As I thought he had come to commend me on quickly informing so many deserving candidates, I proudly reminded him that all the future leaders had been contacted.

Mike then told me that's why he had come to see me. He started by explaining that he had asked for the candidates to be contacted in person for a reason. He then told me a story of a time when he was given a performance review from an executive, who could have easily e-mailed him, but took the time to schedule a meeting. After the face-to-face meeting, in which the executive praised a job well done, Mike said he left the meeting "walking on air."

After that, he said, whenever he had similar, positive news to deliver to someone, he always made the time to talk with them about it in person, especially if it was a significant step in their career, and life, as this was.

I was thunderstruck. I realized that I had screwed up and that I was being selfish. It may have worked out well for me, but not for all the candidates I had called. Sure, they got the news, but Mike was right—how much more special that news would have been if it had been delivered in person.

That conversation changed me for the better. It probably wouldn't have had Mike not taken the time, as he always did, to be open and honest with me. Mike also had a tremendous talent as a leader to frame-up the feedback as a story, including personal experience. This not only made for a more impactful moment but would always assist with my development.

After that, whenever I had similar, positive news to deliver to someone, I made sure it was in person. That moment was transformational.

There's immense value in having a mentor and just as much in becoming a mentor.

I will never forget the first time a peer came to me and said, "I need your advice." "My advice?," I thought. "I have difficulty deciding on value meal number one or three at certain fast-food restaurants." Wow, talk about what many have now dubbed "imposter syndrome."

But, yes, you reach a point in your career when you have amassed enough time and experience that others ask you to call upon it. And you find *yourself* a mentor.

After he posted about mentoring on social media, Christopher and I touched base about what it's like to be on the *other side* of that relationship and *be* a mentor. Again, he summed up being a mentor perfectly.

"If someone asks me to serve as their mentor," Christopher added, "I immediately start asking myself questions like 'What am I committing to?' 'How much time is this going to take?' 'What if I'm not successful in guiding them?' I'm apt to say, 'I just don't have the time.' But if someone tells me they consider me a mentor based on what I've already done, there's no way I'll say, 'No, thank you! Please don't consider me your mentor.'

On the contrary, I'll bend over backward and do whatever I can to help my new mentee."[21]

That encapsulates the importance of being a mentor and the role's responsibility—the mentor has as much responsibility as the mentee.

I realized this during one of the first meetings I had with a newer leader who had come to meet with me. They had asked my thoughts on a situation, and as I started to answer, I noticed that they were taking notes. Something so simple, taking notes in a meeting, takes on a new humbling meaning for me.

This was because now someone was capturing what I was saying and potentially looking to use that advice in their job. There's a great weight of responsibility that comes with that.

As some of these meetings with mentees continued, the weight didn't get any lighter, and it was a sobering thought each time I met with someone as their mentor that I was where so many leaders who helped me were when I first started with the company. Somehow, I had become "the veteran," and with that "label" came the thought that there was wisdom.

For me, that wisdom was all about sharing my journey, philosophy, and stories to illustrate that (good thing I also saved them for a book). I always felt that it was my responsibility to the mentee and, as Christopher said, to do whatever I could to assist them and make sure that they were getting something out of it.

I also learned that mentees need to bring something to these meetings. The very first time I met with a leader that I considered to be a mentor, I fell back on my days as a writer and brought a series of questions to ask, which I was able to break out right at the start of the meeting, when they asked, "So...what can I do for you today?"

I had several meetings with individuals who came to me, and after a few minutes of getting to know one another, I would ask, "So...what can I do for you today?" And unfortunately, there were several times when they would respond, "Well...I wanted to meet with you...I'd like you to be my mentor."

This was usually followed by a few minutes of that ol' awkward silence and eye blinking, after which I would ask

---

21 Christopher White interview with Michael Lyons, October 23, 2022.

some more questions. Many times, that would assist with getting the conversation going…sometimes, it didn't.

This was a learning experience for me, and one that I would pass on to anyone I would hear was going to meet with someone; I would always advise bringing questions and talking points with them—if you have thirty minutes with someone, use all that time.

Every one of those meetings with mentors and every lesson with mentees at Disney still echoes in my mind.

Every one of them taught me so much. I learned that when developing a relationship with a mentor, and you find that person you respect and want to emulate; they should provide an objective voice and sound advice, always have time for you, and provide unbiased information.

As a mentor, I learned the responsibility of all the above is nothing to take lightly and that the mentee is also committed to the relationship.

Ultimately, mentoring is about helping others, which was true at Disney, as we all were striving to be a community and an environment where we were there for each other and would lift each other up.

And, not to steal a page from the script of a non-Disney movie, *The Fast and the Furious* franchise (give yourself another point if you thought that would be mentioned in this book!), but at Disney, indeed, teams became more than co-workers, they became family.

CHAPTER EIGHT

"We Have to Watch Out for Each Other"
The Disney Family

Years ago, like many younger people just starting out, I was struggling financially. My dear mother sensed this, even though I didn't say much about it. One day, in the mail, I received a letter from her.

Two things were in the envelope: one was a check from my mom to me. The other was a small piece of note paper. Written on it, in my mother's handwriting, was simply:

"We have to watch out for each other."

She didn't sign it or write anything else. That's all that was written on it. I placed the note under a magnet on my refrigerator, and it has been on my refrigerator ever since. And, if I moved, the note moved with me and went on my new refrigerator.

It's still there today, a little worn and a little yellowed, but the message is still the same:

"We have to watch out for each other."

Mothers are always right. Mine certainly was. This sentiment has stayed with me and is something I think about quite a bit.

This influenced every part of my life, especially when I started working for the Walt Disney World Resort.

Like many other Cast Members, I pulled up the stakes of my life in another state and moved to Orlando, Florida, to work for Disney. By doing that, I had an opportunity to work in some place I had always wanted to work. However, also by doing so, I had left behind my family in New York, who had been my main support system.

Not long after moving to Florida, there were times on "my weekend" I would realize this. The work week would be taken up with the busyness on Main Street, U.S.A., and interactions with my fellow Cast Members.

My weekend was much quieter. And it gave me time to think: "What if something happens and I need something? What if I am not feeling well? What if my car doesn't start? What am I going to do for the upcoming holidays?"

Like so many working for Disney, my family was in another state and were a healthy car ride or flight away. Who could I turn to?

My fellow Cast Members.

"We have to watch out for each other."

My mom's straightforward philosophy was something that Cast Members lived by. Knowing that so many were in the same situation I was in, Cast Members do watch out for each other. They become an instant support system and eventually transition to something more.

A Disney family.

It sounds like something concocted in a showstopping song from a Disney animated feature, but it's real.

In addition to being so far from hometowns and families, at Walt Disney World, like so many other jobs, you spend a tremendous amount of time with your co-workers and fellow Cast Members.

A bond forms from this time together, and deep friendships emerge—romance blossoms. There are countless stories from Cast Members about how they met their spouses and significant others while working together at Disney. My wife Michelle and I are just one of those many stories.

Part of this strong bond is that most Cast Members have come to work for Disney because they have a tremendous passion for Disney. A large portion of the Cast Member base is like one giant Disney fan convention.

Bringing a large group of people together who have grown up with Disney movies, TV shows, products, and vacations means there will be instant in-depth conversations (geeky, but I mean that in the best sense), in-jokes, and stories about Disney. From that, it's almost like "instant friendships, just add water!"

One shining example of this in my Disney career was in 2003 when I was fortunate enough to be selected as a member of the Traditions team.

That amazing class that started my Disney journey on day one was open for all Cast to facilitate. To make the team, one had to audition and interview through a rigorous, multi-step process.

When you did, you were part of a team facilitating Traditions for all new Cast Members on their first day. You were also part of a team of 34 Cast Members (when I was a part of it) who were so much like you: fans of all things Disney, no, make that, *obsessed* with all things Disney, and they also want to bring all of this to new Cast Members on their first day.

The day after I received the news I had been selected, along with my fellow Traditions facilitators, I started receiving e-mails in my work inbox. It was a distribution list, and some e-mails began circulating around how thrilled we all were to be on the team. Additionally plans began for "after work" activities—"Let's go to a movie!" "Who loves the campfire at Disney's Fort Wilderness Resort and Campground?" "We should all go on a Disney Cruise together!"

I was working as a Disney's Animal Kingdom Coordinator of Training at the time, and my e-mail inbox had never been this active. When I told my co-worker about this sudden influx of e-mails, she said, "Congratulations! It looks like you've just gotten 33 new best friends."

She was right. And, while I haven't remained close with *all* 33 since 2003, a number of them have become more than best friends; they have become a Disney family.

And this is particularly seen around the holidays.

Thanksgiving, Christmas, and other major holidays throughout the year have an extra spark to them when you have a role at Walt Disney World. You become part of many exciting things, especially at those times of the year.

However, particularly for the period of Thanksgiving through New Year's Day, it can be very hectic, as it comprises one of the resort's busiest periods of the year, with Guests striving to enjoy the holiday season during a very compact time frame.

Additionally, as the Walt Disney World Resort is a 24/7 operation, it is open for all major holidays, like many other parts of the service and travel industry. This means that if you work in some part of the operation of the parks or resorts, you are most likely working on Thanksgiving and Christmas Day and other times throughout the year. This is the opposite situation for people in many other jobs and schools, which offer holiday and vacation days, which many use for their Walt Disney World visits.

Enter the Disney Family. During my first Walt Disney World holiday season as a Cast Member, I noticed that many of my fellow Cast would ask me, "So, what are you doing for Thanksgiving?" I thought they were just making conversation, but I soon learned that if I answered, "Nothing much, just working," an invite would usually follow to a fellow Cast Member's house for a full Thanksgiving dinner, either on the actual holiday, the day before, or after.

I became very familiar with the term "Thanksgiving Orphan." According to the *Urban Dictionary*, this is defined as "Someone who has nowhere to go on Thanksgiving because they are far away from family and friends. A Thanksgiving orphan is someone who is taken in by friends or another family to share in their Thanksgiving feast."[22]

It may sound like a sad, almost tragic, and insulting thing to be called a Thanksgiving Orphan, but I found that being one to a Disney Family provided me with some of my life's sweetest holiday memories, shared with astonishingly generous people.

And, this is where the Traditions Family remains close in the (as of this writing) two decades since we first met.

One of the team members, and now one of my best friends, Kyle, held a get-together during our "Traditions year" called "TRADSgiving." On the Saturday before Thanksgiving, Kyle opened his apartment to all on the Traditions team for a full Thanksgiving dinner. This would include music, games, movies, and watching random videos.

TRADSgiving has continued since 2003. It's still held each year on the Saturday before Thanksgiving, and Kyle now

---

22 Urbandictionary.com, (accessed, November 6, 2022).

hosts with his husband, Brandon, in their house, and the list of invitees has grown beyond the Traditions team to include husbands, wives, children, and other close friends.

It still involves a wonderful Thanksgiving dinner, everyone sharing what they're thankful for, and games and videos that have become a part of the Traditions team's, well, traditions.

Even though we are no longer together as a team, and may have gone our separate ways, we still get together for TRADSgiving, and for all of us, it's become our way to kick off the holiday season. For many of us, through the years, it *was* our Thanksgiving, as we would be working during the week. TRADSgiving has now become part of the holiday season for so many of us and one of the things I am continually thankful for each year is *this* Disney family, for sure.

I was fortunate to be an "Orphan" many other times, for Christmas, New Year's Eve, Easter, July 4th, and my birthday, and very grateful for those in the Disney Family who "adopted" me on those days.

And it's also been so nice to invite fellow members of the Disney Family over to our house for the holidays as well. Adding the "leaf" on the table, bringing in the extra chair, and carving a few extra slices of turkey always means that the "family" is expanding.

Disney also looked out for their Cast Members at work, especially on holidays. My good friend, Scott, who worked for many years in Walt Disney World entertainment, fondly remembers a Thanksgiving when he was working at a restaurant at one of the Disney resorts. After closing, the chef and other kitchen Cast Members cooked and served a full Thanksgiving dinner for everyone who worked that day.

The holidays also inspire how leadership creates this supportive family environment. Every major holiday brought celebrations and meals in each area to bring holiday spirit to the workday (everything from barbecues on July 4th to turkey dinners on Thanksgiving was commonplace).

And this sense of family and support wasn't just at the local level. Disney would offer special events, offers, and discounts during the holiday season. In addition, upper leadership would demonstrate how they cared about Cast.

When Cast Members reach milestones in their service with the company, starting with one year and then five-year increments afterward, their area leadership would surprise the Cast Member by gathering the team and presenting the Cast Member with a pin for their nametag, along with a plaque or statue (depending on the milestone). Each one is different, depending on the years of service (see Chapter Eleven for more detail).

Additionally, once a year, the Walt Disney World Cast Activities Team closes Magic Kingdom Park early for Guests and throws a tremendous party at night for every Cast Member who has celebrated a service anniversary that year (in increments of five) from ten years and up.

In addition to parties, Disney Leadership also shows their appreciation in other ways, each day. I saw this first-hand on my last Thanksgiving Day with Disney. That morning, I walked through the Animation Courtyard area of Disney's Hollywood Studios, making my way toward the Grauman's Chinese Theater.

The park wasn't opened yet, and I saw a leader walking from Hollywood Blvd, stopping to shake hands and talk with Custodial Cast Members. It was the Walt Disney World President walking through the park, greeting the Cast, wishing them a Happy Thanksgiving, and thanking them for being there.

He walked by me, probably a good 20 feet ahead, and, as he did, he waved and said, "Hi Michael! Happy Thanksgiving!" I had never met the man before, but he noted my nametag and made me feel like family. As I spoke to Cast during the day, I found out that he stopped and spoke with Cast throughout the park, even making time to go backstage to the cafeteria and stop by Thanksgiving celebrations.

It wasn't just during the holiday season but also year-round that this Cast Member family was there.

As life will do, it can bring us all some challenges and hardships, and whenever this happens, teams would always "rally" with a "What can we do?" or "What do you need?"

If you or a family member was ill, you could always count on your team to be there with you at that time.

In 2007, my mother was very sick, and I was at her side in her hospital bed when my peers, and fellow Training Managers, Scott and Cathy, contacted me to let me know they wanted to stop by the hospital and bring me dinner. Not only did they stop by, but they also sat with me in the cafeteria, had dinner with me, kept me company, and we laughed. I had no family in Florida at the time, so this meant so much to me, as I realized during dinner that I wasn't alone. I am eternally grateful to them.

What Cathy and Scott did wasn't an exception among Disney Cast Members; it was the rule. If a Cast Member was experiencing similar, challenging times, a hospital visit, phone call, or check-in of some kind always happened.

And Cast Members would really "rally" with a capital "R," when sadder times would happen. When I was with World of Disney, a team member's spouse passed away. When word began to spread, and so many discussed how they wanted to attend the funeral, the leadership team partnered with Guest Relations and secured several vans so the team could travel to the services and arrive together. You know, like families will do. It meant so much to the Cast Member who had experienced the loss. The surprise and emotion on their face when we all arrived is something I will never forget.

Speak with so many Cast Members; they have similar, personal stories where others looked out for them and how those moments touched and changed them.

A Cast Member who could no longer afford their rent would be assisted to find a new roommate, or another place to live; A Cast Member who forgot to bring their lunch would suddenly find a meal waiting for them in the breakroom; a Cast Member whose car wouldn't start would quickly find a lift home, or someone to wait for them until AAA arrived.

These situations, and many others like them, all happened. There was never any question, we were all there to watch out for each other.

And, the family coming together wasn't just during times of challenge; the Disney family was also there during life's joyful moments. Many Cast Member wedding parties consisted of bridesmaids and groomsmen who began their friendships as fellow Cast Members working together.

Several engagements, where the couples had met as Cast Members, would take place in the park or resort where the engaged couple first met while working together. Everything from the birth of a new baby to a Cast Member's birthday was a reason for a celebration at work.

But they were all much more than just an excuse to eat another slice of cake in the break room (I know you *Seinfeld* fans are laughing out there); it really was a family coming together.

The now iconic line of dialogue from Walt Disney Picture's 2003 animated feature *Lilo & Stitch* takes on a very personal meaning when you work at Disney:

"'Ohana' means 'family.' 'Family' means 'no one gets left behind.'"[23]

Stitch said it so perfectly. So, did my Mom:

"We have to watch out for each other."

That was a lesson she taught me throughout my life, one that was reinforced when I received her note and one that still resonates with me to this day, as I saw the importance and the impact of doing that when I worked at Disney.

There was always a need *"to watch out for each other,"* come together, and collaborate, at work, outside of work; in so many ways.

---

23 *Lilo & Stitch* page IMDb.com (accessed June 15, 2023).

CHAPTER NINE

The Combined Effort
Collaboration

Three Dog Night was right. One *is* the loneliest number.

For those unfamiliar with Three Dog Night and are thinking they've turned the page to yet another chapter where I've gone off the rails, let me explain and save many readers a trip to Wikipedia.

The rock band Three Dog Night had several Top 40 hits in the late 60s and early 70s. Their single entitled "One" is all about loneliness ("One is the loneliest number that you'll ever do").[24]

The song was about relationships but spoke to how it is genuinely challenging to do anything yourself.

There was someone else, who couldn't be more different than the hippy-sixties sounds of Three Dog Night, who also felt the same: Walt Disney.

Quotes from Walt could be found in countless Walt Disney World backstage locations, prominently displayed in well-trafficked places. The reason was to keep us all connected to his original vision. They were all incredibly inspirational, but one of them was always a constant reminder:

"Whatever we accomplish is due to the combined effort."[25]

Much like the line of the song "One," Walt's quote spoke to the fact that nothing gets done if we focus just on ourselves, but instead, when we look at the "bigger picture" and how we can work together with others.

Collaboration.

---

24 Musixmatch.com (accessed February 10, 2023).
25 "Walt Disney Quotes Archive," D23.com (accessed February 10, 2023).

The entire Walt Disney World Resort is a living example of collaboration, and successful collaboration, at that. The theme parks and resorts can't function each day if all the different teams—attractions, food and beverage, entertainment, merchandise, front desk, housekeeping, custodial—and so many more, don't communicate and work together as one through collaboration.

This seems to make so much common sense; it seems strange to have to write it. Almost everything in the world survives and thrives through collaboration.

But think of those times in our lives, personally or professionally, when collaboration didn't happen. Consider that "gap in communication" or "lack of planning with others," and see if you can recall the results.

They were probably not good. And after the poor results, there was most likely a lot of finger-pointing and "should haves."

Every "How the heck did that happen?" didn't have to happen.

Collaboration, *active* collaboration, even through times of conflict, can save a lot of "Monday morning quarterbacks" from throwing up their arms trying to figure out what went wrong.

Since collaboration is the bedrock of the Walt Disney World operation, I saw it every day. Several stories stand out.

One is from early 2020 and centers on opening the Great Movie Finds shop at Disney's Hollywood Studios. This would be the shop at the exit of the new Mickey & Minnie's Runaway Railway attraction, which was slated to open in March 2020.

Opening day was projected to be extremely busy, as it always was when Disney unveiled a new attraction. Coming off the opening of Star Wars: Galaxy's Edge at Disney's Hollywood Studios just the year before, we felt ready for crowds of any size, as we had seen crowds of *every* size.

But there *was* one concern. Our Great Movie Finds shop, wasn't very big. It only had two registers and was slightly larger than a kiosk you might see at a festival. And, while none of us were industrial or design engineers, we knew it probably wouldn't fit more Guests than my living room.

Opening day would bring with it new merchandise and would also bring with it Guest interest, drawing Guests to our small shop, create one very large queue line...you get where I am going with this.

A queue line takes up space, something we were lacking. We wondered where this line would form and how far it would stretch.

Also, the shop was just outside the exit of Mickey & Minnie's Runaway Railway, where a semi-constant flow of Guests would be passing by. Would the two queue lines intersect, potentially blocking the exit? Would it be the human equivalent of a low front and a high front coming together, causing a storm?

Coupled with this was that the food and beverage team would have a vending cart placed right next to the shop. Would the line for our shop prevent Guests from getting food?

We had visions of Guests wandering around in a giant mass, holding t-shirts and Mickey pretzels, all looking dazed and confused. As a team, we knew two things: 1) We were driving ourselves crazy worrying about what might happen; and 2) We needed to collaborate to stop this worrying.

So, one afternoon, the merchandise, attractions, and food and beverage teams for the area met outside of the construction wall, behind which our shop was taking shape. With us was the Duty Manager for Disney's Hollywood Studios. As mentioned, the Duty Manager served as the point person for the entire park, as a whole. They would look at situations like this holistically, knowing what was best for the area, a specific line of business and for the entire park.

We began to walk the area as everyone discussed their plans for opening day—where the attraction queue line would be situated, where food and beverage planned to have a queue line, and where we, in our small but mighty merchandise shop, planned to have our queue line.

As we talked through this, we realized something: at one point or another during opening day, each of our queue lines *would* run into each other. So, we talked and walked, and talked and walked. We made plans and changed plans.

But when we left the walk, we had a plan, and one in which

no queue lines would intersect. Guests could get where they needed to, safely and efficiently.

The Mickey & Minnie's Runaway Railway opening day was a success. Guests could experience and exit the attraction, purchase merchandise, and get something to eat at the nearby cart without incident. Everything went smoothly.

Because we all took the time to collaborate.

Did my visions of a mass of Guests in front of the shop stop haunting my subconscious in the days before the grand opening? No. Did I worry less about it because we had a plan and collaborated? I sure did.

Some other successful collaborations happened between Disney and other companies who, through an agreement, operate on Disney property. These were termed "Operating Participants."

Some examples include Starbucks, AMC Movie Theaters, and Rainforest Café restaurant. These companies and businesses would operate at a theme park, resort, or at Disney Springs through an agreement. Their goal would be the same as Disney's: to provide a wonderful experience for Guests.

The other goal is that it would be a seamless experience for Guests. Whether it was a Cast Member wearing a Disney nametag, or an Operating Participant wearing the nametag of the company that they work for, Guests shouldn't be able to discern any difference and should receive the same level of service.

That's a big "same page" to get everyone on. How is it done? Collaboration.

This came in the form of something called "Traditions for Operating Participants." Like all brand-new Walt Disney World Cast start their experience with Traditions class on day one, all new Operating Participants start their experience in Traditions for Operating Participants class.

This modified version of Traditions is tailored more toward the Operating Participants. Discussions of Safety, Courtesy, Show, and Efficiency are opened up to the participants to allow them to use examples from their work location.

There's even a discussion about Disney history and the role that Operating Participants have played in Disney history through the years. Jess Rubio started as a caricaturist with Disneyland in 1957 and went on to form the Rubio Arts Corporation, the company that sells balloons and creates caricatures for Guests at Disney and has done so since 1962.[26]

The class was all about bringing the Operating Participants into the Disney family. It was, essentially, a "day one collaboration" between Disney and these other companies, and a collaboration that would continue after, as well.

While working as a Merchandise Manager at Downtown Disney (now Disney Springs), there were several Operating Participants in our area. Even though each had its policies and company philosophies, we all had the same goal to create an ideal experience for Guests.

One of the Operating Participants was a restaurant with which we shared a backstage loading and receiving dock. Each morning, their deliveries would be on one side, and our boxes of merchandise would be on the other.

For several days, we noticed that the restaurant had a large number of boxes, and they were somewhat "overflowing" the delivery area and starting to block our access.

The Cast Members in our area began to get, understandably, frustrated as it continued for almost a week. Honestly, I found myself getting frustrated, as well.

Then, the "they" and "us" started to be tossed around in conversation—"*They* keep doing this to *us!*" A nasty stereotype also started: "Well, you know, if *they* were Disney, this would never happen."

A Business Relations team was in place, and they served as liaisons between Disney and the Operating Participants. There was talk of calling them and "complaining" about what was happening each morning.

During a heated team meeting about our frustrations with the restaurant, one of the leaders on our team asked, "Has anyone gone over and talked to them about it?"

We all stared back at the manager, in a collective moment of stunned stupidity, as none of us had thought to do this over

---

26 Jeff Kunerth, "Jess Rubio: Disney Caricaturist Turned Talent Into A Franchise," *The Orlando Sentinel*, October 24, 2010, orlandosentinel.com (accessed February 14, 2023).

the past several days. I believe someone sheepishly responded, "Uh...yeah...good idea."

It was a *great* idea, and a simple, common sense one, at that. Several of us walked over to the restaurant's back office, moving through the maze of boxes that had now seemed to get bigger. We found the manager, who was a combination of exhausted and exasperated.

Then, we introduced ourselves and let them know we had noticed the larger-than-usual boxes in the back. The manager immediately understood what we discussed and confessed they had been extremely short-staffed. In prioritizing things in their operation, there was no choice but to leave the boxes that could stay in the back.

Short-staffed? Having to prioritize at the last minute and make some tough choices? These were universal challenges. We could relate.

This would lead to our next question for the manager, "How can we help?"

I mean, we could have said, "Good luck with that," but that's not really in the spirit of, ya know, *collaboration*.

The manager graciously didn't want to accept our offer, but then we insisted. They asked if we could spare some extra carts and assist with just helping bring the boxes into their stock room.

We did this and continued to check-in and assist where we could over the next few days, until the restaurant was back on track. By working together, we wound up also building a solid relationship with them.

We worked in collaboration as one team: Disney and Operating Participants, to solve "The Saga of the Crowded Loading Dock." Honestly, if we hadn't collaborated, it would have been a "saga" that would have unnecessarily gone on for too long.

Operating Participants were also a large part of the experience at Epcot when I worked as a leader with the World Showcase merchandise team. The Cast Members who worked in the shops (as well as the attractions and restaurants) in the different pavilions in World Showcase all came from those countries.

The Cast Members on our team were all from France and would come to work for Disney on the international program, coming over to live in Florida for about a year. As they did in each country pavilion, these Cast would serve as representatives of their country and culture.

This would include working in the merchandise shops, such as those in the France pavilion, which comprised several shops that sold perfume and make-up, through a partnership with two major companies.

The eclectic number of fragrances and make-up and the detail of what went into creating all of this were overwhelming. Looking at the perfume bottles and hearing about the creativity and chemistry that went into each, as it was carefully produced, made me feel guilty for just saying, "Wow! Smells good!" each time the fragrance would be sprayed on a card and waved in front of me.

Thankfully, in each fragrance shop, we had representatives who worked for each of the major companies that sponsored that shop. And each of these representatives housed knowledge about the perfumes and make-up in their minds and would be able to share it with the encyclopedic skill that I use to share information about important things, like *Star Wars* movies and Saturday morning cartoons of the 1970s.

Thankfully, for all of us working in the France pavilion, these individuals were very generous with sharing this information. The representatives would take the time with the Cast Members who worked in the shop, to educate them so that they, in turn, could educate the Guests about the product.

Additionally, representatives from the company's main offices would come, from time to time, throughout the year, for product knowledge sessions, which could have also been known as "perfume school."

All of this was so meaningful for everyone: the Cast Members working in the shops had more confidence when a Guest would ask a question, the representatives became part of our team, and the Guests would have a wonderful, immersive experience as they came into the shops, and brought perfume and make-up home as their "tangible memory."

When a Guest asked about a particular perfume, it sure beat relying on my extensive knowledge of, "Wow! That smells good!"

It was an ideal collaboration with ideal results.

I was also on the "other side" of this type of collaboration when I managed the Walt Disney World shops at Orlando International Airport (OIA). As we were in an airport, we had to comply with *their* standards.

They had a team in place, The Greater Orlando Aviation Authority (also known as GOAA—see, Disney isn't the only one who loves acronyms). We had to make sure that what merchandise we carried was within the guidelines of the Transportation and Safety Administration (also known as the TSA, but you probably already knew that).

One time, we had an opportunity to carry a small puzzle that would be perfect for Guests who would be about to travel with children, as it would keep them occupied on a flight. However, it had some sharp edges. So, in the interest of safety, we brought a sampling of the puzzles in to show to our partners at GOAA, so that they could run it past TSA. For completists: we were able to carry it.

Additionally, we also had to abide by "fair and consistent" guidelines at OIA, in regard to everything from inventory space and signage. Disney had just two of a number of retail shops in the airport. If we had the right to do something, it would only be fair to allow others to do that, as well (in fact, in one section of OIA, Walt Disney World's shop is right next to both a Sea World and Universal shop, as the "Trinity" of Orlando welcomes visitors when they arrive).

On top of all the "day-to-day," GOAA fostered an environment of an "airport family." Even though restaurants, fast food and shops were all a part of different companies, the team at OIA brought us all together to collaborate, whenever possible.

This included a monthly recognition program in place at the airport. Travelers passing through OIA had an opportunity to leave feedback on a card, about a positive experience that they had with one of the many employees, and Cast Members, working at the airport.

Once a month, there would be a celebration breakfast for these recipients, and we would have an opportunity to not only recognize the Cast Members working at the airport, but also meet the other teams, from other companies, who were working there, as well. Working at the Walt Disney World shops at OIA was a unique, special, memorable experience and a large part of that was the collaboration from the airport team.

Collaboration also plays a major role in those "I have a great idea!" moments.

I had one of those in spring of 2017. My wife and I spent a vacation at our "happy place," Disney's lovely Vero Beach Resort. One night a week, the resort would host "Pirate Night." Not only would there be an amazing, belt-busting buffet dinner and Goofy and Donald making an appearance dressed as pirates (and wouldn't you think *that* would be enough), but the Cast Members who worked there would dress as pirates and stay "in character" as pirates throughout the evening. Yes, there were plenty of comforting, groan inducing jokes ("What's a pirate's favorite letter?" "Rrrrrrrr!"), but that was a big part of the fun.

After vacation, I returned to my role as one of the managers at the World of Disney with "I have a great idea!" ringing through my head.

A new film, *Pirates of the Caribbean: Dead Men Tell No Tales* was coming to theaters the following month. Naturally, World of Disney was planning to carry a large selection of merchandise tied into the film, but there would also be a great, visual focal point of the product presentation—a large pirate sail and mast emblazoned with the film's logo.

"Wouldn't it be great," I thought, "if some of the Cast Members could dress in pirate costumes, and interact with Guests in pirate 'charact-ARRR' throughout opening weekend?"

I mentioned it to one of the leaders, Rutledge, who had worked at a Magic Kingdom located called "The Pirates League," where Guests could be "transformed" through costume and make-up as pirates.

Rutledge let me know that the Cast Members who worked there would play the part of a pirate throughout, and he let me know that if we were going to do this, we should probably reach out to that team. We brought other leaders along with us on this journey, which would turn out to be an adventure not unlike those that Captain Jack Sparrow embarked on, savvy?

Each and every person that we discussed this with would usually answer with a question, that began with, "You know who you need to talk with...?", which would be followed by another partner that we would need to "loop in" about what we were planning, before we would "raise the sail" on what we were dubbing "Pirates Weekend."

We realized what was needed. Those three words few people like to hear: a conference call.

We arranged a call with everyone from Labor Relations to the Merchandise line of business and from Entertainment leaders to Scheduling. During this meeting, as we went "around the phone," and everyone discussed everything from obtaining costumes to correct pirate phrases, we not only received invaluable insight and input, but everyone who needed to know, was in the know.

After the call, we were able to appropriately "set sail," for the weekend, communicate with the World of Disney team, and "launch" our "Pirate Weekend." It was a huge lesson for me, in these "I have a great idea!" moments: begin communicating and discussing your idea, be open to feedback, and keep widening that circle of communication and input, to all appropriate parties.

The weekend was a fun, interactive experience for, not just Guests, but Cast Members, as well. And, it helped positively impact the business that weekend. At one point, the Cast Members, in their pirate gear, sporting pirate sneers, went out in front of World of Disney, and took a picture. Rutledge printed out a copy of the picture and gave it to me after the weekend. I had it hanging next to my desk each day after, as a reminder of not only how memorable "Pirate Weekend" was, but also how it would have never happened without collaboration.

Sometimes these collaborations are ones that you seek out, other times they come to you.

Once upon a time, there was a movie called *Frozen*. And lots of people throughout lots of kingdoms loved this movie.

When the Disney animated film opened in November of 2013, no one could have predicted the incredible, pop culture explosion it would become, with everyone singing "Let it Go," as the film went on to make $401 million at the domestic box-office. [27]

Because no one predicted *Frozen* skyrocketing to such success, it was a challenge to keep merchandise from the film on store shelves. At the time the film opened, I was a leader with Once Upon a Toy at Downtown Disney (before it transformed to Disney Springs), and I remember as I would come in each morning, I would see a line of Guests waiting for World of Disney to open for the day, all of them just hoping for the chance that there would be some Anna and Elsa merchandise.

I remember receiving not one, not two, but three different e-mails from peers and partners I had worked with in the past that began something like, "My daughter absolutely loves *Frozen*, does your shop, by chance, carry any merchandise from the film?"

By the time January and February of 2014 hit, the requests for the product, and how quickly it was heading out the door as soon as it hit shelves, became a daily occurrence.

Then, in March of 2014, *Frozen* was going to make its debut on DVD, and every parent's "nightmare" of watching the film over-and-over-and-over was about to become a reality. As the release date of the DVD got closer, there was talk that there would be a "release party" at Downtown Disney, to commemorate it.

I thought, of course, with World of Disney being the "hot spot" for all things *Frozen*, that would be where the release party would be, until our General Manager, Suzette and our Project Manager, Lisa, let me know that they would be entrusting this event to Once Upon a Toy.

On the outside, I smiled and said, "Great!" but, not going to lie, on the inside, my mind was…well…frozen.

I had an image of hoards of Olaf aficionados camped outside the shop, like fans waiting for concert tickets.

That image would never come to be, but instead, "The *Frozen* DVD Launch Party" that March of 2014 at Once Upon a Toy was a rousing success, thanks to a number of individuals coming together, in a short span of time, to make sure that we had an event that was on par with Elsa's coronation.

---

27 *Frozen* page, Wikipedia.com (accessed June 20, 2023)

As demand for *Frozen* product was still far outweighing supply at the time, our partners within the Merchandise line of business secured items, to make sure that shelves would be full that day.

The Disney Events team, whose job it was to constantly operate events like this (and on a larger scale), assisted with helping to create a plan for Guest flow, and secured a "photo-op" featuring a statue of Olaf, against of a snow-covered backdrop. Additionally, the Events team also allowed for a television, flocked in "snow" to be placed in the shop, so that the Cast Members could have a "Let It Go" sing-a-long with Guests throughout the day (follow the "bouncing snowflake!").

The stock team ensured that the boxes of DVD's arrived on time and were placed strategically throughout the shop (it's nice to have DVD's for a DVD launch party, ya know?).

Other lines of business even joined in to support, with Entertainment connecting with a DJ who would play songs and invite Guests to dance, just outside the shop, creating a "party" vibe, and food and beverage kiosks offered *Frozen*-themed snacks and drinks.

Additionally, the Labor team worked closely with us to make sure we had the right staffing (it takes a village to have a sing-a-long!), and the Duty Manager walked the shop with our leadership team to discuss what the possible impacts would be for all of Downtown Disney.

Wrangling all of this, and keeping it all organized, moving forward and constantly communicating was Project Manager, Lisa, and General Manager Suzette, who were the lynchpin to guide "The Frozen DVD Launch Party" to its debut.

And, on launch day, there *were* Olaf fans eagerly waiting outside, but they weren't camped-out like concert goers, they were excited families who cheered when we opened the doors. What followed was a day filled with "Let It Go" playing on repeat (I still feel the need to apologize to all parents there), photo after photo with Olaf, a non-stop dance party, and plenty of *Frozen* DVDs and merchandise finding a good home.

As one of the stock Cast Members clocked out at the end of their shift, they said to me, "Today was a lot of work, but I haven't had this much fun at work in a long time."

And none of that "*Frozen* fun" would have happened without the collaboration that made it happen.

The ol' saying, "you can't live your life in a vacuum," is so true. There's a reason that vacuums suck. Trying to accomplish anything, especially on a grand scale, is complex and can often be impossible.

I saw this first-hand in one of the other areas where I worked as a leader. As a management team, we had planned and decided on a new process for our closing procedures each night. From that, we wrote our standard operating guide and picked a date to implement this.

We then met to inform the Coordinators and other Cast Members in the area about this new process. As we discussed the process, I noticed blank stares around the room.

When we finished, hands began to go up, and each question asked seemed to start with either, "What about…?" or "Have we thought about…?" As the leaders began to take notes, we realized that we would need to go back and revise the process we wanted to put into place and delay the date that we wanted to start it.

As we closed the meeting, we asked if anyone had anything else to add. One of the Coordinators simply said, "I wish you had come to us when you were planning this."

They were right. We should have. After that, anytime I would be a part of planning any new initiative, I would always ask, "Who else should be involved?"

Each day brought a new lesson like this about the power of working with others. There may be conflict and differing opinions when we collaborate, but that is all a part of it.

Collaboration brings new ideas, helps share a challenge, and opens possibilities.

We Walt Disney World Cast Members could see just how essential this would be, especially during the most difficult of times.

CHAPTER TEN

Storm Season
Creating Magic During Challenging Times

When Disneyland opened in 1955, there were no newspapers for sale inside the park, which was also true when Walt Disney World opened in 1971 and has been since (with the exception of hotels, which offered some periodicals). This was to deliver Walt's original vision for Guests to leave the "real world" behind and truly become immersed in the park's fantasy.

Strange to think that, today, newspapers have become an antiquated thing of "the past" and that the "real-world" news is available all the time, in the palm of our hands with our phones. However, it's still something that Guests like to put aside and genuinely get "lost in Disney."

But sometimes, that "real world" encroaches on the escapist realm of Disney.

Unfortunately, it's unavoidable. Those "real-world" events are sometimes just too difficult to now look past or around. Guests hoping to escape to some magic at Disney may have difficulty focusing on that magic as that "real world" infringes on the fantasy.

It happens for Cast Members, as well. And there have been several times they have had to put on a "brave face." Their role of doing all they can to "create happiness" and preserve that magic can sometimes hit significant roadblocks, as hearts and minds are torn between facing certain real-world events and helping others find refuge.

This happened during the week of June 12, 2016. That night, a gunman entered the Pulse nightclub in Orlando (not far from Walt Disney World property). The gunman killed 49 people and wounded 53 others.

Sadly, this was a tragedy that gained national attention. It especially rocked the local and Walt Disney World communities. Many Cast frequented the nightclub, and two of victims had been Cast Members.

As everyone still reeled from this horrific event, just two days later, on June 14th, a young two-year-old Guest was attacked and killed by an alligator in the water near Disney's Grand Floridian Resort and Spa.

It was unreal—that so much that was so bad could occur in such a short period. This time became so heartbreakingly pivotal that when Disney CEO Robert Iger penned his memoir, *The Ride of a Lifetime*, he wrote about the events' profound impact on him in the book's prologue.[28]

I was at the World of Disney shop at the time. We had just experienced a grand re-opening, in which Downtown Disney became Disney Springs less than a month earlier, but that positive celebration of accomplishment seemed so far away now.

A dark cloud hung over every day after, as everyone, both Cast and Guest, walked around in a daze. It was challenging to focus on work, knowing that these terrible events had just happened. The coverage on the news and social media was a constant reminder. One of the challenges for us as Cast Members was that it was also on the minds of all the Guests who came into the shop.

There were several moments during the week when Cast Members had to excuse themselves and go backstage to cry. It was one of the few moments in my Disney career when I didn't know if I or if we as a team could continue to go on each day providing goodwill during such a time.

Luckily, the executive leadership team also knew this; honestly, they felt the same way. One afternoon, they gathered the Disney Springs leaders in a conference room.

We didn't know the specifics behind the meeting but knew it was related to the Pulse nightclub and Grand Floridian events.

As we gathered in the room, the executives came to the front and began to set the stage, letting us know that they had brought us together to check in and see how we were all doing,

---

[28] Robert Iger, *The Ride of a Lifetime*, (New York, Random House, 2019), pp. viiii-xxiii.

how the Cast was, and how the Guests were doing.

As one of the executives began to tell a story of a Guest they had encountered, they became emotional and had to stop. They were feeling what we were all feeling, in that it was so difficult to find the words, and when you could, you just couldn't get the words out.

The executive eventually finished and opened the floor to questions. Afterward, we could stay longer in the room to talk with each other and have a conversation.

It was an incredibly impactful meeting, and later, I thought of the words of commentator Eric Sevareid, who spoke quite eloquently on *The CBS Evening News* the night that Walt Disney passed away on December 15, 1966. Among his comments, Mr. Sevareid said of Walt:

> "He probably did more to heal or at least soothe troubled human spirits than all the psychiatrists in the world. There can't be many adults in the allegedly civilized parts of the globe who did not inhabit Disney's mind and imagination for at least a few hours and feel better for the visitation.
>
> It may be true, as somebody said, that while there is no highbrow in a lowbrow, there *is* some lowbrow in every highbrow.
>
> But what Walt Disney seemed to know was that while there is very little grown-up in a child, there is a lot of child in every grown-up. To a child, this weary world is brand-new, gift-wrapped; Disney tried to keep it that way for adults…
>
> By the conventional wisdom, mighty mice, flying elephants, Snow White and Happy, Grumpy, Sneezy, and Dopey-all these were fantasy, escapism from reality. It's a question of whether they are any less real, any more fantastic than intercontinental missiles, poisoned air, defoliated forests, and scraps from the moon. This is the age of fantasy, however you look at it, but Disney's fantasy wasn't lethal. People are saying we'll never see his like again."[29]

This was Eric Sevareid's way of saying that all that Walt gave the world was necessary. And that, in every way, was why we gathered with our executives during that difficult week in June of 2016.

---

29 Bob Thomas, *Walt Disney: An American Original* (New York, Hyperion, 1994), p.355.

The innocent world of Disney seemed so far away, as if invaded by all the dread of the real world. Gathering as we all did that afternoon at Disney Springs, as many other Walt Disney World teams did that week in different ways, allowed us to see that our job was to continue what we did each day. We knew after that conversation, fireworks, parades, attractions, as well as greetings, conversations, and laughter that were part of our day, were needed at that time more than ever.

We all also knew that, by doing our jobs, we were in no way diminishing the events that happened that June. They still left a scar, and we continue to, and still do, think of them.

But, our role was to, as Mr. Sevareid said, "heal or at least soothe troubled human spirits."

Those two events were just one time that the "real world" collided with the fantasy we were to provide. Another major collision that left both Cast and Guests reeling occurred about twelve years prior when all of us in Central Florida became very familiar with two words: "storm season."

Before the fall of 2004, it had been about 34 years since Central Florida had experienced a hurricane.[30] That all changed, in August and September that year, as we made up for "lost time" with three different hurricanes coming through the area. *The Tampa Bay Times* dubbed them "The three-eyed monster."[31]

In a weird meteorological moment, each one was three weeks apart, and in a very unmagical way, each storm impacted the Walt Disney World resort and the surrounding community.

In an ironic twist, Walt Disney had chosen Orlando because of its location inland. A location near the coast would have made the resort more vulnerable, and the "land-locked" location near Orlando seemed like a safer bet.

Hurricane Charley felt otherwise.

This wouldn't be the first time a hurricane would impact Walt Disney World operations. On August 31, 1985, the resort closed at 5:00 pm, due to Hurricane Elena, and on August 2,

---

30 Eric Burris, Charley Made Landfall 18 Years Ago in Florida, wesh.com, August 13, 2022 (accessed June 21, 2023).

31 Joe Mario Pederson, "The Year 3 Hurricane Paths Crossed One Spot in Central Florida, Tampabay.com, Sept. 24, 2019 (accessed November 22, 2022).

1995, there was a delayed opening due to Hurricane Erin. Both storms resulted in no significant damage.[32]

These storms also brought no significant operational impacts. Then came September of 1999 and Hurricane Floyd. The storm was making a beeline for the Vacation Kingdom of the World, but, at the last minute, the hurricane veered north out over the water, eventually striking Cape Fear (ironically), North Carolina.

While it was making its projected path right into the middle of Florida, Walt Disney World Emergency Management and executive leadership decided to close the theme parks early in advance of the storm. When Floyd turned north, that same team decided to re-open certain sections of the Resort now that it was safe.[33]

That happened just before my career with Disney began. In the days leading up to Hurricane Charley's arrival in 2004, many that I worked with who had been there for Floyd seemed sure that this would be a repeat.

Hurricane Charley was initially thought to weaken as it passed over Cuba, but instead shifted West and gained strength. It was believed that it would make landfall in the Tampa Bay area, but rather, it caught many off-guard, shifted, and roared across the state of Florida, right through the Orlando area.

You may be thinking that Weather Channel's famed meteorologist Jim Cantore has ghostwritten this section of the book. However, there is a reason for all of this detail. The impact of Charley on the Orlando area and the Walt Disney World Resort was devastating.

As Cast Members always do, we rallied to get ready. I was at Epcot then and remember the search during the days before the storm to get all loose items that were backstage put away. Additionally, any outdoor locations onstage, such as merchandise carts, had to be secured to withstand wind.

When the Walt Disney World closing was communicated, we had to ensure all Cast received appropriate information

---

[32] Jim Korkis, "WDW Chronicles: When Hurricane Floyd Came to Town," Allears. net, September 25, 2022 (accessed November 30, 2022).
[33] Ibid.

regarding the closing, re-adjust schedules, and provide contact information for Cast to call (and an emergency phone number) for details on re-opening.

We were all a Disney family, so there was a lot of discussion with the Cast to ensure *they* were taking proper precautions at home and that they weren't going to spend the hurricane alone or knew where their nearest shelter was.

Despite the closing, there never once was there a moment of "We can't do this." Or even a "How are we going to do this?" Instead, there was "We will figure this out" and "Let's find a way." Through this unknown was a communal Cast Member spirit of getting through this together.

This was much needed, as it was also an exhausting time. Once the Walt Disney World Resort was readied for the impending storm, we then had to go and secure everything at our homes.

It's a good thing all that securing was done. On August 13, 2004, at approximately 9 p.m., Hurricane Charley arrived in the Orlando area as a Category 1 storm, with wind speeds recorded at 105 mph at Orlando International Airport.[34]

I was at home, "hunkered down" (a term that became part of so many Floridians' vocabulary). As cliché as it may seem, Charley roared through like a freight train.

I was one of the fortunate ones who never lost power, but as cable went out, I watched coverage of the hurricane on a small, battery-operated TV. As the local meteorologist discussed Charley and its location, it was as if she was discussing the arrival of a motorcade. "Lake Buena Vista, Charley will be coming to you in about ten minutes, and then, Orlando, you're next..."

Sure enough, right on schedule, the winds started like a jet engine taking off from the roof of the house...but this jet didn't fly away; it just kept revving and revving its engine as the sound of debris hit the windows and roof. It was like being in some strange submarine, knowing something was going on out there in the pitch black but not being able to see it.

---

[34] Joe Mario Pederson, "'Nightmare Scenario': 15 Years Since Florida Was Beaten, Bruised By 4 Hurricanes In 6 Weeks," *Orlando Sentinel.com*, August 13, 2019 (Accessed December 13, 2019).

Then, on the tiny black-and-white screen, the blob of the radar moved away. And, with a sigh of relief, there was the realization that we had made it through. Then, there was another realization that, in the light of the next day, there would be the first glimpse of what Charley had wrought.

The *Orlando Sentinel* reported:

> Charley caused $14 billion worth of damage and was directly responsible for the deaths of ten people in the United States as it made its way north toward South Carolina. One of the casualties was a 5-year-old girl from Orange County who was killed after a vehicle had been blown into the car she was in...[35]

This devastation took its toll on Walt Disney World property, as well. As I was fortunate to still have power, the traffic lights in my area were still working, and I lived close to the property, so I could safely get to work the next day.

As it frequently is after a storm, the next day was a beautiful one. I drove backstage behind World Showcase at Epcot; I was shocked at the debris: tree limbs, leaves, and puddles were everywhere. But, when I eventually walked on stage, near the Italy pavilion, I was stunned by what I saw: it looked as if the hurricane had never happened.

Across the property, Disney had enlisted a "ride-out crew," leaders who had made the selfless decision to stay at the park, in a safe location, for hours on end so that when the storm passed, they could begin assessing, cleaning, and getting ready for Guests.

As Charley swirled out to sea, Epcot was opening in just a few hours, and we were ready—*entirely* ready.

Lee Cockerell, who was the Executive Vice President of Operations at the time, recalled the day after Hurricane Charley in his book, *Creating Magic: 10 Common Sense Leadership Strategies from a Life at Disney*:

> The next morning, we opened on time. And the families who poured in were astonished to find the sunlit theme parks looking spotless and the operations running as if nothing had happened. What they could not see was the massive teamwork behind the scenes that made it all possible or

---

35 Ibid.

the stress and fatigue behind the smiling faces that greeted them. While many other attractions and businesses in Central Florida remained closed and local municipalities were struggling to restore power and clear the roads, Disney was making magic.[36]

Tremendous effort went into creating this magic during such a time. While the ride-out crew and those who arrived that morning in the parks cleaned and assessed damage to make sure that the park could, once again, be ready, at the resorts, where Guests had to "hunker down," the show went on.

Since the Resort hotel Guests were spending a lot of time in their rooms, the staff ensured that they had enough food as the storm came through. The Resort teams also partnered with the Entertainment team, so that many Disney characters would appear in the lobbies during the quieter, safer times. This helped to add an element of calm to the proceedings and also allowed Guests to have some semblance of the Disney vacation that Hurricane Charley had taken away.

When Epcot opened the day after the hurricane, the park looked as it always did on the quietest of days, pristine, with the Disney element of escapism firmly in place.

This didn't come easy. Residents of Florida didn't have power for weeks after the storm. It was reported that 22,000 residents still had no power at the end of the month. Many of these were Cast Members.

As they always do, Disney did much to help their "Disney family" during this rough time. Whether it was the food and beverage teams handing out bags of ice to those who were in need, or fellow Cast inviting others without power for a much-needed hot shower and air conditioning, it was an inspiring time of "watching out for each another."

Despite their lack of power, hot water, and tree limbs blocking their driveways, these Cast made it to work at Walt Disney World. And by doing that, so many could escape the "real world" that Hurricane Charley had brought to Walt Disney World Guest and Cast.

---

36 Lee Cockerell, *Creating Magic: 10 Common Sense Strategies From A Life At Disney* (New York, Doubleday), 2008, p.3.

At the end of that day after the storm, there was undoubtedly a greater sense of satisfaction and relief. Sadly, that was not to last. As we always did at Disney, we began to look ahead and make plans, but Mother Nature had her own.

As August began to end, meteorologists began to talk about "another disturbance that's out there." And, as they pointed to these cloud masses and blobs of color on their maps, they began to broach the topic of "We may have another hurricane heading our way."

"Nooooooo!" we all thought collectively, along with "There's no way," "This can't happen," "It isn't possible," and even the very generous, "It will probably head somewhere else. It's someone else's turn."

They were all the ultimate shouts of denial.

We found that out on September 5, 2004, when unbelievably, just three weeks after Charley, Hurricane Frances made landfall in Florida at Hutchinson Island on the southeast coast.

At Disney, this meant a complete replay of everything we had done several weeks prior: prepping everything to withstand another storm, changing schedules, and putting plans together for re-opening.

Most of the Cast were still bearing the "scars" from Charley: blue tarps on roofs that were damaged, plywood still on windows, and many had just gotten their power back or were still without it.

All the Walt Disney World Cast Members took a collective, weary, deep breath, said, "Here we go again," and went back into full "hurricane mode." We all had an uneasy sense of deja vu as we prepped before the storm. On a somewhat small, positive note, all the preparations came a lot easier this time (probably because we had just done all this three weeks earlier).

Frances was different in that this storm decided to take its time. While Charley was a mercifully quick visitor, Frances moved very, very slowly. At one point, it just spun off the coast. With this reduced speed, Walt Disney World was forced to close for two straight days.

But, as with Charley, the parks opened the day after the storm passed. Cast Members, weary on the inside, smiling on the outside, were once again ready to help provide Guests with the dose of Disney that Hurricane Frances had taken away.

In the days that followed the passing of Frances, we looked ahead, once again. I was in a meeting, discussing plans for the upcoming busy holiday season, when someone in the room said something along the lines of, "Hey, did you hear? It was on the news that they're tracking another potential hurricane."

We just stared back at them, blank stares of disbelief.

And just a few days after sporting these blank stares, we were back preparing Walt Disney World Resort for another hurricane. This one would be named Jeanne. This time, as the hurricane led as the top story of all local news reports and consumed every conversation, there was less denial and more of what could be best called "exhausted disbelief."

Sure, we placed the sandbags by all the doors at work and pulled in all our patio furniture at home, but we all did it with catatonic expressions. We were all hungover from a party we didn't want to attend. One that seemingly wouldn't end.

Jeanne arrived, on September 26, once again at Hutchinson Island, just east of Stuart, FL. Once again, Walt Disney World closed, and just as the Cast Members had done two times prior in less than two months, they made sure that the Guests were well taken care of while at their Resort during the storm and made sure that the parks re-opened, looking as they always do, once the storm had passed.

When hurricane season 2004 ended, there was a collective sigh from all of Florida followed by a collective, "Are we sure?" Another hurricane, Ivan, also hit Florida that September but didn't come close enough for a Walt Disney World closing.

Sometime after, as part of the many "thank yous" provided by Disney's executive leadership team, there was a token of recognition given to all Cast Members. It was a pin that featured Mickey Mouse, bracing against the wind, and holding tight to his iconic hat from *Fantasia*'s "The Sorcerer's Apprentice." It was on a card that featured a map of Florida and a large "Thank You" at the top of the card.

Under this was written:

"Nothing can stop us from delivering the magic…Not even hurricanes Charley, Frances or Jeanne." Below that were the dates of each storm.

Sure, easy to dismiss it as "just a pin." But, after everything we had been through, that image of Mickey defiantly standing up to the storm, coupled with the sentiment that the three storms didn't stop the Walt Disney World Cast, meant so much.

So many of us who took tremendous pride in everything that we did each day, knew that we were upholding a tradition that Walt had started with Disneyland, as stated on the plaque at that park's entrance: "Here you leave today and enter the world of yesterday, tomorrow and fantasy."

Leaving that "real world" behind was sometimes difficult, especially when that "real world" sweeps across Walt Disney World in the form of three hurricanes.

Unfortunately, 2004 wouldn't be the last time hurricanes would impact Walt Disney World operations. As of this writing, significant hurricanes in 2005, 2017, 2019, and 2022 have also interrupted Walt Disney World operations.

But thanks to that unforgettable August and September of 2004, Cast Members are now fully prepared for this experience. As that small but memorable pin said, nothing can stop them from "delivering the magic."

Just three years before that season of 2004 hurricanes, the world was reverberating from events that forever changed us.

September 11, 2001.

So many have stories about that day and the time after. Here is mine:

I had been living in Florida for about a year. It was my day off, and I had slept a little later, looking forward to a nice, relaxing day. After turning on the news and seeing what was happening, I realized that my mom, who was still living in New York, worked on Broad Street in New York City, which was not far from the World Trade Center.

I called her office. After several attempts where no one picked up, she finally answered, told me she was fine and that they were evacuating the building. She said she would call me when she got home.

My Mom's average commute time from Long Island to Manhattan each day was approximately an hour. It took her almost nine hours to get home that day.

When she finally called me that evening, I was tremendously relieved. The story of how she got home that day was terrifying and unnerving and could fill a chapter itself. But it was also filled with moments of kindness, like the deli owner who gave out free drinks to her and others. It was filled with bravery, like the firefighter who helped my mom onto a boat so that she and others could get to Brooklyn, to get a train home. She always remembered them both and talked about them every year around September 11th.

My Mom felt highly fortunate. She made it home. I felt very extremely fortunate that she made it home.

It was and still is heartbreaking that many others didn't. Having the day off was both a blessing and a curse, as it meant an entire day to watch and re-watch the horrific, unbelievable events of the day over and over.

Later that night, I gathered with some fellow Cast Members I worked with on Main Street, U.S.A. We came together because we all had the same day off and spent the day feeling isolated, lonely, and helpless. As we talked and tried to make sense of the day, the conversation eventually turned to the fact that we would return to work the next day at Walt Disney World.

As we returned for our Magic Kingdom workday on September 12, 2001, we heard stories of what had transpired the day before from our fellow Cast Members who were also there that day. We heard that an announcement was made that the park would be closing. We were told about what it was like when all the Magic Kingdom Guests left at the same time. There was also much confusion as to why the Park was closing in the middle of a picture-perfect weather day.

Cast Members who had been watching on TVs in break rooms or hearing about it from their peers knew. In the days before smartphones, Guests were unaware as they rode It's a Small World. Cast that day struggled with sharing information and simply tried to reassure Guests that due to "unforeseen circumstances," the park was closing, as they made sure everyone exited safely.

Those who were there after the Guests left told us how eerie and uncertain it was to look out on deserted Main Street, U.S.A., up toward Cinderella Castle, not fully knowing all that was going on themselves until they got home from work and, like the entire world that day, sat in front of their television.

Then came the days after, where, as Cast Members, we all made valiant attempts to keep the magic going while a fog of continual grief descended on each day.

This seemed to be true of the Guests, as well, many of whom were "stuck" at Walt Disney World, their vacations extended. At any other time, this would have been cause for celebration, but given all that was going on, you could tell by the look on their faces that there was a feeling of guilt at being at this most joyful place at such a tumultuous time.

There was that same guilt for me as a Cast Member. Strange as it may sound, I found it difficult to be pleasant to someone during such an unpleasant time. Plus, I had no idea what Guests were going through or how they had been affected, and I didn't even know if I should be smiling at them and providing a cheery "Hello!" as they entered the shop.

Talking to my fellow Cast Members in the break room and cafeteria as the non-stop news coverage played on the TVs nearby, I found out that many felt the same way. And many who were far away from home began to have thoughts of moving back and being closer to family.

Our manager, Mike, must have sensed this. One night, after we closed, he gathered us all together for our usual nightly meeting. During it, he talked about how he could see we weren't the same; he admitted that he wasn't the same, and, like us, he could see that the Guests weren't the same.

He then proceeded to tell us how much the Guests needed us at this time and how much we needed each other, as well, to remember what Disney means to the Guests and us.

I tried after that. Honestly, I did. One night, after work, I came home, and as I sat down, I was relieved to see that *The Late Show with David Letterman* was on. It was so nice to see "regularly scheduled" television again after many days of news coverage of the September 11th events.

It was his first show since that day, and David Letterman did a wonderful job of somberly guiding the audience, and himself, back into the show. I remember, at one point, during his very touching and eloquent opening remarks, he said, "It's terribly sad here in New York City. We've lost 5000 fellow New Yorkers, and you can feel it, you can feel it, you can see it, it's terribly sad, terribly, terribly sad..."[37]

Watching the show did nothing to help me. It just made me miss New York and all my family there.

I continued to "sleepwalk" through work. Oh sure, I remembered what Disney meant, but, like everyone, I felt so preoccupied. David Letterman's words kept echoing in my mind, "terribly sad," "you can feel it, and you can see it." That sadness in New York City was with us all, as each day continually took on a mournful tone.

Then, one day, there was a turning point that touched me and so many others who were there and helped me see what my manager Mike meant.

Each day, just before dusk, there is the flag retreat ceremony in town square in Main Street, U.S.A. It happened and still happens each evening. Walt Disney World Security Hosts and Hostesses come into the square, and they lower and fold the flag. Everyone is invited to join in and say the Pledge of Allegiance and in singing "The Star Spangled Banner."

This ceremony was, and is a Magic Kingdom institution, but after September 11, 2001, it took on special significance. What few Guests there were in the park, along with all Cast Members that were in the area, would stop and come out to participate.

It was always accompanied by tears, and even more so on one day.

Donald Duck appeared on Main Street, taking pictures and signing autographs. As the flag retreat started, he was with a young boy, and as the music began, Donald took the young boy's hand and signaled for the boy to imitate him in saluting. Donald then turned toward the flag as he held the young man's hand, and the two saluted during the entire flag retreat ceremony.

We all talked about that indelible image for some time, and, for me, it became emblematic of Disney. I had only been a Cast Member for about a year, but I had a realization, just as in difficult times in the past, even a Walt Disney World visit and the

---

37 Speakola.com, September 19, 2001 (accessed January 4, 2023).

escape it provides is needed for many, and as a Cast Member, our role was to deliver upon that.

"We Go On" was the song played during the Epcot nighttime fireworks show, "Illuminations," at the time, and in its melancholy way, it seemed fitting. Like so much else, Walt Disney World continued but changed. Security bag checks are the biggest of these, where all Guests must stop before entering a Disney Park.

But, the Guests all did it, and continue to do it, to have someplace on the planet to visit, where a gentle, simple moment like Donald Duck holding a young child's hand can make things better, at least for a short time.

In the years that followed September 11, 2001, Walt Disney World life continued in the "new normal," a term that we all became very comfortable with, as that refuge for so many Guests.

Years passed, and, as Cast Members, we would often reflect and remember that time around the fall of 2001. During those conversations, we often hoped we would never have to go through something so terrible again.

Then came March 2020.

Yeah. Just say the year 2020 and it immediately conjures up so many unpleasant memories of what has been dubbed the "worst year ever."

Information about this thing called "the Coronavirus" began to appear on the evening news in late 2019 and into early 2020. It was a contagious disease caused by a virus and could cause fever, cough, and breathing difficulties, among other symptoms. It was also linked to a number of deaths.[38] But it was in China. So far away.

I was at Disney's Hollywood Studios at the time, and all of that seemed to be happening in the background. It was a record-breaking year and one of the busiest holiday seasons, I can remember. The attraction, Rise of the Resistance, opened in early December of 2019 in Star Wars: Galaxy's Edge, bringing with it throngs of Guests eager to experience it (and get in the brand-new "virtual queue" system that had just started).

---

38 COVID-19 page, Wikipedia.com (accessed January 9, 2023).

This collided with the already busy end-of-year Christmas through New Year week.

We all went into January 2020 exhausted but exuberant at having such a successful season. As Walt said, we kept "moving forward" to what was next: the opening of another new attraction, Mickey and Minnie's Runaway Railway.

The eagerly awaited new addition would be taking the place of The Great Movie Ride, and my team was going to be responsible for the opening and operating of the merchandise shop located just outside the exit of Mickey and Minnie's Runaway Railway, (which would be named "Great Movie Finds").

January and February of 2020 became a blur of meeting and planning with all key peers and partners, such as Merchandise Planning, Visual, Stock, Industrial Engineering, Labor, Training, and even other lines of business, and the park Duty Manager.

As we continued these meetings, checking off on our list what was done and what was going to need to be done—walking areas to find appropriate stock space, planning for where to place a queue line of Guests for opening day, and getting the first "sneak peek" at the product—news about "this Coronavirus" began to infiltrate more of the conversation.

In January, we learned that Shanghai Disneyland and Hong Kong Disneyland had closed over concerns about the virus. But, again, it was so far away. We had a new attraction and a shop to open.

By the opening day of Mickey and Minnie's Runaway Railway, in the early days of March, as many came to congratulate the team, we all refrained from hugs, high-fives, and handshakes. Talk of Purell, handwashing, and sneezing into the crook of one's arm also became part of work conversations.

A week after the opening, I traveled up to New York, with my father, on a planned vacation to visit family. During that week away, the "wheels fell off," and it all seemed to happen in one afternoon as I went to the grocery store with my father, and we noticed all these customers leaving with their carts overflowing with toilet paper and paper towels.

That was the same day I learned that the NBA was canceling the remainder of their season, the new James Bond movie's opening was delayed, and Broadway would go "dark" for about a month.

That day, while in New York, I also learned that Walt Disney World would be closing "for two weeks."

Looking back, I was oblivious and so innocent, and when I have talked to others since, we all seemed to feel this way.

I flew home a few days after on an almost empty flight. As a state of emergency had been declared, and air travel was such a part of the conversation (especially international flights), I didn't know if I would be able to fly home.

But I did and didn't know what I was coming back to. All I knew was that we would be "working from home."

As it was for so many, this was such a strange time for all of us working at Walt Disney World. We were used to going in each day and getting everything ready and open for Guests, keeping everything running smoothly throughout the day, and then closing it up until the next day. Now, all the parks and resorts on the property were closed, with only a skeletal staff to maintain them.

We were operators; we were used to running, you know, an operation. Now, we were working on those "back burner" projects at home as we became increasingly familiar with this thing called a "Zoom Call."

A few weeks earlier, we had been discussing the best process for stocking the new shop at Mickey and Minnie's Runaway Railway and making plans for how busy it would most likely be during the Easter break. Now, we were staring at each other in these little *"Brady Bunch* boxes" on our computer screens and putting together plans for re-opening the park.

And, as time passed, we didn't know when that would be. Working from home all day allowed constant access to the news, which wasn't promising, and was very, very scary and unnerving, as we learned more and more about a new term that would become part of our everyday lexicon, "Covid-19."

In connection with that, we also soon learned about another word, "Furlough." As projections for Covid-19 became more dire, Walt Disney World leadership eventually decided to keep the resort closed (save for that skeletal staff) and place most of the Cast Members on furlough until it was safe enough to re-open.

Those on furlough would remain active Cast Members, retaining our benefits, but we would not receive a paycheck until the appropriate leadership team contacted us. But we had no idea when that would be.

"Into the Unknown," the song from *Frozen II*, which had just bowed into theaters four months earlier, seemed to be the theme for how everyone felt. On a Friday in mid-April of that year, we logged off our computers, plugged our work phones into chargers, vowed to keep in touch with each other…and went on furlough.

Walt Disney World Resort eventually re-opened in July 2020, and Guests, in smaller numbers due to social distancing, came back that very first day. The emotion of being back brought tears streaming down their faces, which could be seen, just above the masks they were wearing.

Just as they had before, Guests showed how much they needed the happiness that Disney provided, especially during such an unhappy time.

Before we went on furlough, one of my peers, Steve, shared an e-mail that had been forwarded multiple times and made its way to us.

The e-mail had come from the Guest Communications Team, and it was from a Guest who began the letter by informing us that their husband was an emergency room nurse on the front lines of the COVID pandemic.

The Guest let us know that their husband said that the first thing he wanted to do, as soon as they were able to, was to go to Walt Disney World. To provide incentive, the couple posted Walt Disney World pictures on their wall and had already begun planning their trip.

The Guest then went on to say that they couldn't imagine what we were all going through and told us not to worry, as they and other healthcare professionals would all be returning someday for a Walt Disney World visit.

The Guest concluded the letter by saying that they were focused on the day when they would pose in front of Cinderella Castle.

So, the family of a *nurse* during the COVID-19 pandemic was sending an inspirational message to *us*, the Walt Disney

World Cast? What more motivation did we need to keep our hopeful eyes on the future?

Being a part of Disney during all these most challenging times, from September 11, 2001, through the pandemic, showed me how much Disney means to Guests. My friend James says that we *need* Disney, and his saying is, "If there weren't a Disney, we would have to create one."

Additionally, being there for Guests and each other as Cast Members during these difficult times taught me a lesson about the impact of what we do in life. We may not even realize it and, at times, discount what we do, personally and professionally, but we need always to remember that we are making a difference for someone.

Those newspapers, still not available in Walt Disney World theme parks, wouldn't always provide good news, be we Cast Members really could. That meant we had a place on the shoulders of Disney's rich history.

CHAPTER ELEVEN

The Light Is Still Burning
When Disney History Came Alive

The next time you visit Disneyland in Anaheim, California, before you run to the Indiana Jones and the Temple of the Forbidden Eye attraction in Adventureland, stop at the Fire Department on Main Street, U.S.A.

Look up at the window above the firehouse, and you will notice a Victorian-style lamp and light glowing. Inside is the apartment where Walt Disney would stay during Disneyland's earliest days. Walt knew that he wouldn't be able to commute to Anaheim constantly and would need a place to rest. The apartment would also house the Disney family, when they visited.[39]

When Walt was in the apartment, the light in the window would be on so that all would know that Walt was there. After Walt's passing in 1966, the lamp has remained on. In 2020, Disneyland's President Rebecca Campbell commented on the significance of this:

> "Inside Walt Disney's apartment overlooking town square at Disneyland, a light has shone through the window above the firehouse for decades. It glows as a source of inspiration to our Cast and Guests as a remembrance of the man who once looked out that window to the sights of happy families making memories below."[40]

Paging all fellow "Disney geeks!" Just reading that, just knowing about that light, and just seeing it at Disneyland, you

---

[39] Sophie Jo, "A Second Home: Walt Disney's Fire Station Apartment," waltdisney.org, June 20, 2020 (accessed on January 10, 2023).

[40] Jessica Figueroa, "PHOTO: Lamp Remains Lit in Walt Disney's Apartment at Disneyland During Extended Park Closure," wdwnt.com, April 1, 2020 (accessed on January 10, 2023).

can feel the legacy of Walt Disney and the rich history of the company that he founded, which bears his name.

Working as a Walt Disney World Cast Member, there were times that I could feel this legacy and times when Disney history would come alive. Oh sure, as with any job, there were days when you would get caught up in what was happening at the moment. But then, there were those times when you would realize the history around you.

It was always much needed, came along at just the right time, and served as a perfect "re-set." These moments of historical realization also came along at the most unexpected times, many times during simple conversations.

While working as the Magic Kingdom Merchandise Training Manager, I was meeting with one of the Area Managers, Martin. Before meeting with Martin, I was told that he had been with Walt Disney World since its opening.

While in his office, I noticed that Martin had the famous *Life* magazine from Walt Disney World's opening in 1971 framed on the wall. "Disney World Opens" was splashed across the cover photo of a large group of Cast Members assembled in front of Cinderella Castle.

As I stood closer to the photo, I half-jokingly asked Martin, "So...where are you?" Without missing a beat, Martin stood up, walked over to the framed magazine, pointed at the group, and said, "That's me, right there."

I was dumbstruck. Martin was displaying his usual humble nature. But, for me, the moment was much more. I was very familiar with the *Life* magazine issue hanging on Martin's office wall and had stared at that cover many times; now, I knew someone in that picture. During this meeting, where we were about to discuss Cast Member training, it was the realization that Disney history was all around me and that some fellow Cast Members were a part of it.

Whenever possible, like so many, I sought out conversations with Martin to absorb his wisdom and hear him share the stories of his role as part of Walt Disney World's growth through the years.

As Cast Members, we would wear service pins on our name tags. These would signify the number of years that you had been with Disney, starting with year one and then in five-year increments after that. Each gold pin in the corner of the nametag would feature the year in number and a Disney character or icon.

Mickey as Steamboat Willie is on the one-year pin, Pluto is on five, and it went on from there. For the higher years of service, there was Donald for forty and both Walt and Mickey indicating 45 years. There's now even a fiftieth-anniversary service pin that features Snow White and a fifty-fifth pin featuring Mickey with a paint pallet and brush, as the statue given 55-year Cast is Mickey and the gang painting a portrait of Walt.

As Cast Members, whenever we would see those service pins with those double digits that were of a higher number we hadn't seen before, it immediately sparked conversation. Almost all of these were an inquisition for the owner of that service pin to find out what Disney history they had seen and been a part of.

From these questions, I heard stories: My leader, Mike, who told of a *Star Wars* and Disney connection in the late 70s, long before the Walt Disney Company had acquired Lucasfilm. In the summer of 1977, not long after Mike started with the company, when the very first *Star Wars* film debuted, he recalled how the Lake Buena Vista Shopping Village (now Disney Springs) featured an appearance by Darth Vader as a photo-op for Guests who were discovering this new film. Quaint beginnings for what is now a much larger part of Disney.

A Cast Member I worked with on Main Street, U.S.A., told me about their first job with Disney as a third-shift Security Host, whose responsibility was to watch over the construction site of a new park called Epcot, scheduled to open in 1982. He told me about watching Spaceship Earth grow from a hollow metal shell.

One of the Disney's Animal Kingdom leaders I worked with shared humorous tales of attempting to operate the theme park on opening day, April 22, 1998, while *Good Morning America* and *Live with Regis and Kathie Lee* were broadcasting from the brand-new park.

And one of my favorites was a story told by my leader Dru about when he was a manager at the Emporium, and he served as a personal shopper for Princess Diana after they had closed the shop to the public.

So many other stories I was lucky to hear and listen to, like a fireside chat, each one of them weaving a tapestry of the unfurled history. As each story went on, my bug eyes widened as I acted more and more like comedian Chris Farley on the classic *Saturday Night Live* skit, "The Chris Farley Show," where he would simply respond to every celebrity guest, "That's awesome!"

There were also multiple times I had the opportunity to walk through Disney history, literally…with Disney Imagineers!

While working as the Magic Kingdom Merchandise Training Manager, we would host a new leader orientation program. As part of this, several Imagineers, the creative team responsible for designing, maintaining, and refurbishing the parks and resorts, as well ensuring that the stories there are told as they should be, would come and walk with the group of new leaders.

Another part of being an Imagineer was to stay in touch with operations. The purpose of this relationship was to see how they could assist with supporting the show and making sure that the intended story was being told as Walt and the original team of Imagineers had envisioned it.

For a good part of the day, we would be able to spend time with several Imagineers, who would not only ground us all in the history of Imagineering but would take us on a Magic Kingdom walk, discussing the stories in each land, as well as details that we may not have been aware of.

I had the chance to be a part of this while hosting the Imagineers for the leadership orientation at the Magic Kingdom and as a participant when I went to work at Epcot and Disney's Hollywood Studios.

The anecdotes, the specifics, and the history flooded my Disney-thirsty brain, and I ate it all up like a Dole Whip on a July afternoon!

And don't think I don't recall some of these facts that I still let slide into conversation while visiting parks with family and friends, acting as if I'm the font of all knowledge who just graduated with his degree in Disney. Of course, as soon as a family member or friend sees their favorite character, my short lived "fame" disappears.

Of all the wonderful information I was lucky to hear on those early morning walks through those three Disney parks, we had all to ourselves pre-opening, these are some of my favorite slices of Disney history:

On a Magic Kingdom morning, when the fog hung low over the Park, the Imagineers shared with us the history of two significant statues in the park. One is entitled "Partners" and is a now iconic statue of Walt Disney and Mickey Mouse holding hands and standing in the hub in front of Cinderella Castle. The other statue, entitled "Sharing the Magic," is of Walt's brother Roy O. Disney, sitting on a park bench, holding hands with Minnie Mouse, in town square, by the flagpole at the beginning of Main Street, U.S.A.

Both statues were created by legendary Imagineer Blaine Gibson, who began his career as an animator and then went on to help create some of Disney's first and most famous theme park attractions.

In addition to both statues being beautiful, emotional tributes to the two men who founded one of the world's most famous companies, the Imagineers shared a subtle, artistic message behind both statues.

"Partners" features Walt, not just holding Mickey's hand but also gesturing down Main Street, U.S.A., pointing Mickey toward some distant or not-so-distant horizon. According to the Imagineers, this signified that, just as Walt is leading Mickey in the statue, Walt was also leading the company.

Additionally, Walt is gesturing toward Roy's "Sharing the Magic" statue, in which Roy holds Minnie's hand. The Imagineers invited us to look closely at that statue and notice that Roy's hand is underneath Minnie, signifying the support he not only always provided to Walt but also how he supported the company after his brother's death in 1966.

This is an incredible, touching detail to notice and reflect on the next time you are on Main Street, U.S.A., with thousands of your newest, closest "friends" as you wait for fireworks.

Another Disney history detail discovered thanks to a walk with Imagineers was at World Showcase at Epcot. As each country's pavilion was built to reflect real locations, the Imagineers knew they had to keep a timeless feel. The decision was made that the architecture of each country's pavilion would be pre-World War II. There would be no contemporary touches so that each would be "frozen in time" and not remind Guests of the "outside world."

Another "real-world" location that the Imagineers had to bring to life was a "...Hollywood that never was and always will be," as stated on the dedication plaque at Disney's Hollywood Studios, which opened as Disney-MGM Studios Theme Park in 1989.

In bringing the Hollywood Boulevard of the 1920s through the 1940s to life as Guests enter the theme park, the Imagineers provided details that could find you spending a decent portion of your day just seeking them out.

One of these details is at a shop that many may walk by or through on their way to the rest of the park (or even rush by if your group is boarding for Rise of the Resistance). Next to Celebrity 5 & 10 is the shop Adrian and Edith's Head to Toe. While it may seem like a generic name, as with so much at Disney, there is a story and history behind it.

The shop is named after two legendary movie costume designers from Hollywood's Golden Age. Adrien Greenberg (known simply as Adrian) designed hundreds of costumes for MGM, including those in 1939's *The Wizard of Oz* (yup, the iconic ruby red slippers were designed by Adrian).

The other half of the shop name belongs to Edith Head (get it "...*Edith's Head* to Toe."). Head is arguably one of the most famous costume designers in motion picture history, winning eight Oscars for her work on films such as *White Christmas*, *The Ten Commandments*, and *Rear Window*. Additionally, Head's unique style and appearance influenced that of the character Edna Mode in Disney and Pixar's *The Incredibles* and *The Incredibles 2*.

I still remember these and other facts and would have never been aware had it not been for the time spent with the Imagineers. When each session was over, and they would ask for any questions, it was difficult not to raise my hand repeatedly. There's a thirst for Disney knowledge and appreciation for the time the Imagineers took to share Disney.

I was also lucky enough to do the same and pass on this history to others. For a brief time at Disney, I facilitated the Disney's Youth Education Series Program. This was also called the "Y.E.S." series. Disney loves a good acronym, and this *is* a good one.

Like Traditions, I taught these sessions on a "cross-utilization" basis. I kept my full-time job at the time with Disney but would be "borrowed" when the schedule required me to facilitate one of the Y.E.S. sessions.

These programs were offered to elementary through high school students during their Walt Disney World visits. The subjects ranged from world history to science and involve taking a medium size group of students and their chaperone on a tour of one of the Disney theme parks, using different settings and attractions to illustrate and educate the students.

Somehow, after auditioning, I was chosen to facilitate one of the Y.E.S. programs' science sessions. Those who chose me must not have seen my high school report cards, but I was thrilled to fill in any scientific gaps I missed in eleventh grade as I doodled in the margin of my Trapper Keeper notebook.

The session focused on light and rays, and I found out during training, that we would have an opportunity to take the class on a brief, backstage tour of The Haunted Mansion.

It was difficult to hear or learn anything new after that because all I kept hearing was "backstage tour of The Haunted Mansion." We would get to walk in through a backdoor and share a little about what it takes to bring "999 Happy Haunts" to life.

It was all about sharing the concept of "Pepper's Ghost." No, this isn't some sort of strange condiment that disappears when you use it; it's an illusion, a magic trick of sorts, that's been used in several venues, like theater, concerts, and theme parks, since 1862. British scientist John Henry Pepper created it.[41]

The illusion involved utilizing a reflection—when an image is reflected on a transparent screen at a 45-degree angle; it allows that image to have depth and seemingly appear in another area. Think about staring out a window to your front yard on a sunny day. You can see both your front yard and your

---

41 Pepper's Ghost and John Henry Pepper pages, Wikepdia.com (accessed January 14, 2023).

own image staring out, which seems to be "floating" over the front yard.

That lovely little scientific fact there seems like a perfect Double Jeopardy question, but what does this have to do with The Haunted Mansion? Before we go any further, let me just say, "spoiler warning!"

As I have said, I never want to ruin the magic and take it away from any Disney fan and Guest. What follows doesn't precisely do that; it essentially explains how Walt and his Imagineers created magic. However, if you believe in those 999 ghosts and have always dreamed of being number one thousand, please skip to my story about the American Adventure at Epcot.

For those daring souls, jump into the "virtual Doom Buggy" with me.

A backstage glimpse of The Haunted Mansion would begin by educating the students about Pepper's Ghost (to illustrate the session's light and ray's topic) and then letting them know that this illusion is used to bring the famed ballroom sequence of The Haunted Mansion to life.

For those who have been at the attraction, you may have wondered how do dancing and dining spirits in the ballroom look so "see-through" as you whirl by on your Doom Buggy?

Pepper's Ghost, that's how.

The ballroom scene has giant, floor-to-ceiling panes of glass in front of it; the attraction vehicles (Doom Buggies) pass by on the track on the other side of the glass, and below the track are animatronics of the ghosts with lights shining on them, which causes a reflection in the glass and the result is the ghostly appearance that Walt and his innovative team of artists were going for.

As Y.E.S. Program facilitators, we were responsible for (and had permission to) bring the class into a backstage door of the attraction and quietly stand under the track, next to the animatronics that were casting reflections in the glass. We, of course, had to be careful, and stand in a specific spot, moving not a hair. If our reflection accidentally appeared on the glass, we would inadvertently become one of those ghosts. The Guests riding by in the cars above would be confused at how some geeky-looking guy and a junior high school class ended up in the ballroom.

After we left and headed back out on stage, not only was the concept of Pepper's Ghost fully illustrated, but the students, and their teacher, would seem as slack-jawed and buggy-eyed at this peek behind the Disney curtain as I was.

Now, each time I ride The Haunted Mansion, I can't help but think about those students and their amazed expressions during the times I stood under the Doom Buggy track, went back in time in Disney history, and learned that no one should be afraid of Pepper's Ghost.

There was also a moment when Disney history came to find me. One hot summer day, while working at the American Adventure pavilion at Epcot, my peer and I noticed an older gentleman walking through the pavilion who seemed to be looking for something.

One of the attraction hosts, Lonnie, went over to talk with the gentleman and let us know that the Guest's name was Dallas McKennon. I immediately thought, "Why does that name sound familiar?" I was soon about to find out.

Lonnie let us know that he was an actor *and* a prolific voice actor, at that. McKennon had provided the voices for several animated characters, including several Disney features like *Lady and the Tramp*, *One Hundred and One Dalmatians*, *Mary Poppins* and *Bednobs and Broomsticks*. He also narrated and played roles on over a dozen Disney records. McKennon was a part of TV shows like *The Archie Show*, and he was the voice of Gumby.

Gumby?!? Here at the American Adventure pavilion?!? Yup, and we soon got the opportunity to meet him. As it turns out, McKennon had also done many voices for Disney theme park attractions, including that of Benjamin Franklin in the American Adventure. And McKennon shared with us that he had never seen the show.

That was about to change. Thanks to kindness from the American Adventure attractions team, they made sure that McKennon could watch the show for the first of what would be multiple times that day.

Before one of the shows, McKennon was also introduced and invited up to the podium at the front of the theater, where he said a few words to the Guests, and even borrowed Lonnie's glasses to imitate Ben Franklin.

That evening, I met a friend for dinner. He told me he had quite the day and asked me about mine. I told him that I had met and spent a portion of it with the actor who provided Benjamin Franklin's voice for the American Adventure. "Well, you've got me beat," my friend admitted.

Such was working for Disney; the company's amazing history was always a part of our days.

And a shining example of this was a team that would uphold this like heritage corps: The Walt Disney World Ambassadors. As stated before, the Ambassador program began in 1965, with the very first Julie Reihm, and would eventually continue in all parks.

Becoming a Walt Disney World Ambassador or an Ambassador at any of the Disney Parks involves a rigorous audition and interview process open to all Cast Members. Once chosen, it is a full-time job for two years. Not only do the Disney Ambassadors serve as representatives for the company at media events and take part in interviews for television, radio, and other outlets at significant events, such as opening a new attraction or resort, but they are representatives for Cast Members, as well.

The Ambassadors would come to Cast events, including celebrations of Cast service anniversaries (recognizing their years of service with the company). During these events, the Ambassadors would make a speech, thanking the Cast Members for all their hard work and connecting the Cast Members to all that Disney represents.

During these times with the Ambassadors, with their lineage to the first Ambassador, Julie Reihm, you could *feel* Disney's history as a part of the moment. Their presence always connected us to why we worked for Disney.

I was lucky enough to get to know several Ambassador team members, and they've become friends, making this connection even more special. Meeting a Disney Ambassador is like meeting a part of Disney history, *ongoing* Disney history, and just one of the many moments, while working for the company, when there would be a sense that Disney history came alive.

The lessons that I learned while being lucky enough to be a part of these and other moments when Disney history seemed to unfold all around me was that we all need to take time to connect with our own history and recognize how far we have come, both in our personal and professional lives, as well as remember why we are on the path that we are on.

That lamp, burning day and night in the window of Walt's apartment in Disneyland, sheds light on all areas of the company and helps illuminate the way for all Cast Members... even during their most challenging times.

CHAPTER TWELVE

"If We Weren't So Down, We'd Up and Leave"

Personal Challenges and Learning from Mistakes

While working as the Magic Kingdom Merchandise Training Manager, my leader gave my peers and me some advice. She told us that if we were ever invited into a meeting, and there was a box of tissues sitting in the middle of the table, be aware that the meeting probably wasn't going to go well, as the person holding the meeting was obviously anticipating tears.

On March 24, 2009, I was called to a meeting, in a conference room, where a box of tissues sat in the middle of the table.

My leader was right; it wasn't a good meeting. During it, I was informed by the executive and human resources manager that my position was being eliminated and, unfortunately, I was being let go.

It was one of those instances that so impacted my consciousness I don't remember much of the meeting after the initial shock. I recall handing over my company ID and my Blackberry (that dates this story, doesn't it?!) to the HR manager and them walking me to my office so I could get my things.

It all seemed to be happening at some low-volume distance. I don't even remember driving home (be glad you weren't anywhere on the road near me that day).

When I got home in the middle of the morning, when I was used to being at work, I felt like I was "playing hooky" or taking a sick day. As the day went on, I received phone calls from my peers updating me on others who had been subject to the same fate, or calling me to let me know they had been let go, as well.

At lunchtime, several of us who suddenly found ourselves with a free day gathered at the social and gastronomical epicenter of the area, the Orlando Ale House. We arrived for lunch, stayed for dinner, and left well afterward.

All day long, the same question kept being asked, "How could this be?" It was one of those "bad dream" days, and I thought I would soon wake up. But, as the day and the orders of Chicken Zingers at Ale House went on, we collectively realized it was all too real.

Just about six months prior, on September 29, 2008, the stock market crashed in what was heralded as the most significant drop since the Great Depression.[42] Even if you didn't closely follow the stock market back then, you knew the word "crash" wasn't good.

A recession followed, and in uncertain economic times, people second guess if they should take a vacation, and if you're the "Vacation Kingdom of the World" at the Walt Disney World Resort, that's not good.

Like so many companies, Disney never wanted to do this. Some tough decisions had to be made, and, unfortunately, reducing its workforce was one of these. And sadly, for me, I was part of that workforce that was reduced.

When I woke up the following day, after a night's sleep that felt more like a night's nap, for a brief minute, I thought I was late for work and was about to go into my morning routine. Then, I remembered. I didn't have to go in today... tomorrow... or the day after...or...well, you get it.

I poured myself a much-needed cup of coffee and sat out on my apartment's screened-in lanai. I stared out at the complex and noticed how quiet it was. Sure it was; everyone else was at work.

I started to get sad. A lyric from the song "Not in Nottingham," from my favorite Disney animated feature, 1973's *Robin Hood*, began to run through my head:

"If we weren't so down, we'd up and leave."

I thought about that guy that was me who, nine years prior, had driven for two days from New York to Orlando

---

42 Kimberly Amadeo, "The Stock Market Crash of 2008," thebalancemoney.com, May 25, 2022 (accessed on January 18, 2023).

with dreams of working at Disney. I began to think about that dream being over and that it would soon be time to start anew somewhere else.

After a few minutes and a lot more coffee, I thought again. And I don't know why, but my thinking began to change. I suddenly realized *This wasn't my fault. This is no one's fault.*

The people involved in the decision making at Disney didn't want to do this. It wasn't like Mickey and the gang were hanging around his house in Toontown and said, "Hey, gang, you know that guy, Michael Lyons? He loves Disney and his job so much and is doing it well. We should get rid of him. All in favor say, 'Oh boy!'" No.

If the Market had soared the previous fall, and people were clamoring to plan vacations, things would have been much different. Once I realized this, I couldn't be bitter. That would just be a tremendous waste of energy. It's okay if others want to be, but not me. There was no one to be bitter to or nothing to be bitter about. My feeling about Disney had not changed. I still had the same strong positive feeling about Disney that had been a part of me since I was a kid.

Feedback about my performance from my leader had been very positive. It wasn't me; it was just the challenging times we were in. To quote *The Godfather*, "It's not personal…it's strictly business."[43]

I started to feel better, but then I thought about the whole "starting over" thing again and having to look for a job. "Where is my resume?," I thought. "Wait, do I even *have* a resume?"

Then, somehow, another thought came to me: *Sometimes, starting over is a good thing.*

I suddenly realized that amid all this unpleasantness, I had an opportunity to write my future, which can be very good. This was the circumstance that I was in, and everyone started telling me, "My job now was to find another job." What was to come was all in my perspective, and I made a pact with myself right then and there that I would be optimistic about whatever was to come, and I would try to reevaluate and learn. I was free to take an honest look back.

---

43 *The Godfather* page, IMDb.com (accessed June 23, 2023).

An experience from four years earlier occurred to me: a great opportunity that I had completely screwed up.

In the spring of 2005, I was offered a "temporary assignment" as a manager with the Traditions team at Disney University. These temporary roles were very commonplace at Disney. If one team member were transitioning to a new, temporary role, or a project with an end date, someone would need to take over their responsibilities while on a temporary assignment.

One of the managers with the Traditions team would be segueing to a new role, but only for several months, and, having worked with the leadership team during my time facilitating Traditions, I was very fortunate to be offered the opportunity to serve as a temporary backfill for the manager, while they were away.

I was working as a manager with Merchandise operations, at the time, at Epcot, which meant that someone would have to backfill me (there was always a "domino effect" when it came to these temporary assignments). However, the leadership team at Epcot was very supportive, as an opportunity to work at Disney University and be a part of the Traditions team was indeed a golden one.

I was very excited to be offered this and to get started. It would be a very different world. Now, instead of serving as a front-line manager at Epcot, working opening and closing shifts during weekends, holidays, and evenings, as well as in all sorts of weather, I would be the front-line manager in a building and of classes.

It was fun, especially since I was on the leadership team responsible for the first day for all new Walt Disney World Cast Members and leading a team of Traditions facilitators who shared tremendous passion for Disney. Additionally, I was part of the team while we were auditioning new Traditions facilitators. Having gone through that process, it was fascinating to be on "the other side" of it.

Traditions is a big part of Walt Disney's history and vital to every Cast Member's experience, and each day at Disney University was a flashback to my first day with Disney, and there was always a pleasant feeling of comfort walking into the building.

Like any job, a manager with Traditions is also hard work. Responsibility for a Cast Member's first day and their experience brought a lot with it. The days when College Program Cast Members arrive would flood Disney University with several hundred new Cast Members, all of them lost and wondering what would come next.

We also had to ensure that Cast met "Disney Look" guidelines, had time to meet with Union representatives, received their nametags, got lunch, and that classes didn't run too long or too short. On days when we had no classes, the management team would facilitate other classes, work on projects, and make future plans with script revisions and continual training for the current facilitators.

Some days, Disney University felt as busy as Epcot on New Year's Eve. It was all new to me, and I started feeling overwhelmed. I felt that I was struggling to grasp some things. It seemed to take me longer to "catch on."

I should have asked for help. I didn't. The leadership team I worked with at the time and the leader I reported to were all so lovely and supportive. Looking back, other than the fear of admitting I was struggling, I don't know why I didn't. I should have.

Every job and new experience have times of adjustment. It is okay to have a bit of "homesickness" for the job that you just left. I wasn't considering any of that. Instead, I foolishly thought, "I will soldier on. After all, it's a temporary assignment, and I will be back at Epcot in a few more months."

I was playing "fake it 'till you make it," years before that phrase was "a thing."

My leader must have sensed this. After about two months, they asked me, "So, how's it going?" As I stammered through my response, attempting to put on a brave face, I found myself saying, "...I mean, I do miss my old job."

My leader knew. They were a good leader and could tell that I wasn't putting my heart into what I was doing. The worst and most embarrassing part was that it was reflected in my performance, which wasn't as good as it could have been.

After several conversations with both my leader and their leader, where to make matters worse, I went "back and forth" about how I felt; we agreed that I would end my temporary assignment early. I went back to my previous role as a merchandise manager at Epcot.

While all this was happening, I remember a phone call with my dad and telling him what was going on. I embarrassingly admitted that I wasn't looking at the job at Disney University seriously enough. As I struggled, I saw it as "just temporary" and wasn't "giving it my all."

"You know what your job is?" my dad asked. "Whatever you are being paid to do and whatever you are responsible for."

He was right. I was embarrassed. We all have those growing pains at a new job, and others are there to help us if we ask. I should have known that; I should have done that.

For some time after, I "beat myself up" over what happened and would play out things differently, sometimes wishing for a time machine to go back and do it all over again and do it correctly. I would make myself crazy wondering what my life and career would have been like had I done my job better.

But, as time passed, I realized there was no going back, only moving forward. The only thing I could do would be to ensure that I never did this again. We can't often control the events in our lives or at work, but we can control how we react to them and take responsibility for our actions.

And do the job we are "being paid to do" and do "whatever you are responsible for." It's just like a scene in *The Lion King*, in which Rafiki hits Simba on the head with his stick. As he rubs his head, Simba, the lion, asks, "What was that for?" Rafiki's response: "It doesn't matter. It's in the past."

"Yeah," Simba says, "but it still hurts."

Rafiki notes, "Oh yes, the past can hurt. But from how I see it, you can either run from it or learn from it."[44] At that point, Rafiki swings his stick again. This time, Simba ducks his head.

It was a most difficult time for me, but when life would "swing the stick" at me again, I would be ready to duck. That's what my mistake taught me.

About a year after my time at Disney University, fortune shone on me again. I was offered another temporary assignment as a Training Manager at one of Disney's resorts. "Wow!,"

---

44 *The Lion King* (1994) page, IMDb.com (accessed June 23, 2023).

I thought, "How lucky am I? I am interested in training and development and have been meeting with several leaders in that organization, and I am offered this opportunity!"

Then, the Training Area Leader offering me this opportunity told me that the job would be the Front Desk and Housekeeping Training Manager at Disney's All-Star Resorts.

Wait. *What?!?*

I explained that my background was in Merchandise operations, and the leader told me it didn't matter. They were interested in my leadership experience and my interest in and passion for training.

But Front Desk and Housekeeping? I had never even considered that, except when I checked into a resort and returned to my resort room at the end of the night. Not only that but Disney's All-Star Resorts, themed to sports, music and movies, was a big, high-volume busy location.

I accepted, but I could feel myself slipping back into those overwhelming feelings I had before.

As part of my preparation for this new role, I was scheduled for in-costume training, working at All-Star Resort's front desk and with the Housekeeping teams. Working the front desk and checking Guests into their rooms during a hectic morning was daunting, and blessings to my patient, veteran trainer, who took the time to walk me through everything. To me, the computer system used seemed as if I would need Stephen Hawking to explain it to me. I got through the day, and somehow, each Guest was successfully checked into their room.

I was getting overwhelmed again.

Then, I trained in Housekeeping with an excellent, hard-working Cast Member who had been with Disney for some time. In an eight-hour shift, not only did I make beds, vacuum, dust, and do many of the tasks associated with housekeeping (and seemingly none of the tasks I do at home), but I also had to unclog both a toilet *and* a bathtub.

Extremely overwhelmed, that was me!

Here I was, just learning this role, so how in the world would I support Cast Members who were training in this role? I could feel those same angst-ridden, foolish feelings that raced through my mind coming back to me.

Then, I heard my dad's words returning to me again: *You know what your job is? Whatever you are being paid to do and whatever you are responsible for.* Temporary or not, it was my job and needed to be taken seriously.

Like Rafiki hitting me on the head, I realized I had to learn from my past.

Just as I had done in Merchandise, I would support the Cast any way I could, realizing that even though these Cast weren't stocking shelves and working at cash registers, their expectations of their leaders would still be the same.

As I didn't know a lot, I also asked questions. *A lot of questions.* "Now, explain to me what that is?" was my favorite. What was so overwhelming was that there was so much I didn't know, and I had to fill in those blanks.

Two months into this temporary assignment at Disney's All-Star Resorts, I was offered a "statused" or permanent role as the Magic Kingdom Merchandise Training Manager.

In my last meeting with the Area Manager, he was candid about the fact that he didn't know how "a merchandise guy" was going to adjust to the "resort world," but he was extremely nice when he said that after just a few days, these concerns were gone, I had exceeded his expectations and he had received very positive feedback from the All-Star Resort team.

Additionally, on my last day, I was approached by one of the Cast Members who had reported into me during my brief time at the resort. He was a long-term Cast Member, very forthright with his opinions and not easy to win over. He came up to me as I was leaving and said, "I'm sorry to see you go...I actually liked you."

In my head, I was laughing hysterically. In my heart, I took this as a rave review from a tough critic.

It was a brief time at All-Star, but I will always treasure it. Not only was the team there supportive and created a fun atmosphere, but I felt, in some small way, I had "righted my ship." I had changed my perception; I had taken my dad's advice and done my job.

This change in my perspective – looking at the possibilities and the challenges of what would lie ahead and knowing that I needed to do what I could to meet them both – helped me in the days, weeks, and months after I was let go from Disney in 2009.

Were there "down" days? Were there days when I felt hopeless? Were there days when I did nothing but watch reruns of *The Golden Girls*? Yes, to all the above.

But allowing myself those days also allowed me time to decide what to do next. One thing I knew for certain — I wanted to return to Disney. And I actually did return to a Disney job in June of 2009, as a part-time merchandise manager at Epcot.

Honestly, this was challenging. It wasn't how I wanted to return to Disney (I tried to come back full-time, and I hadn't worked in the operation for several years), but it was my job, Rafiki kept hitting me on the head, sparking me to learn from my past.

I stayed focused, and about six months later, thanks to my leaders' support, I transitioned to full-time again as a manager in the exact same location. Shortly after that, my leaders worked with me and helped me develop and grow, and through their support, I was promoted two years later to the role of Area Manager.

On the day my promotion was announced to the team at Epcot, I remember reading the e-mail announcement sent out, and I couldn't help but reflect.

It had been three short years since I had been let go. So many times, in my life, I had heard about how hard work, remaining focused, and positive thinking can yield good things, but, honestly, I often thought that was just the stuff of those inspirational "Hang in there, baby" posters. I now knew it was true.

It reminds me of a line from Disney's first direct-to-video movie, 1994's *The Return of Jafar* (another reference no one may be expecting). There's a scene where Jafar is about to enact his revenge, and the Genie says, "Don't worry, Abu. He's a genie, and genies can't kill anyone." Jafar then shoots fire at the Genie, and the burnt Genie responds, "But, you'd be surprised what you can live through."[45]

---

45 *The Return of Jafar* page, IMDb.com (accessed on January 26, 2023).

Indeed. While not attacked by an evil former vizier-turned-genie, I learned a lesson that you can surprise yourself with what you are capable of, even against daunting odds.

I learned this again in 2020, when the COVID-19 pandemic upturned all our lives.

Like so many companies, the Walt Disney World Resort was forced to shut down from March through July of 2020, with most of the Cast Members placed on furlough.

When the Parks and Resort Hotels re-opened, Cast were called back to work. However, because not all locations would be re-opening, not everyone was called back. Those who weren't remained on furlough. I was one of those who remained on furlough during one of the strangest periods of my life.

They had resumed Walt Disney World operations, and this was a big part of the local news each night, but I was home. Waiting. It was a time of limbo for me and so many others. Each week, you'd wonder if this was the week you would get the call to come back. Then, the week would pass.

Luckily, at the time, my schedule was flexible. There were no significant plans for my future beyond, "Do I clean out the closet this week or clean out the garage?" Or, "Boy, if I get called back, I will have to go through a twelve-step program to wean myself off CNN."

Then, the summer went by, and news about the virus was, in no way, getting better. It was just the opposite.

On Tuesday evening, September 29, 2020, I received a call. An executive at Disney and an Human Rresources Manager were on the other end. While there was no table and no box of tissues, I still knew the call wasn't good.

I was informed that my position was being eliminated, and I was being let go again.

I would joke about it days after with peers and friends (many of whom were in the same boat), and I'd say, "Well, I guess I didn't do that right the first time because I've got to do it again."

Humor was a defense mechanism, having been through this situation just eleven years prior, I felt as if I was prepared for this to happen again someday, potentially. Seemingly after the

"IF WE WEREN'T SO DOWN, WE'D UP AND LEAVE" 159

phone call, I had a moment not unlike that morning in the spring of 2009 when I sat out on my lanai.

I once again was out of a job, which many people, unfortunately, go through, but, once again, I had an opportunity to write, or re-write, my future, which few people ever get the chance to do...especially twice.

Again, I had no bitterness. COVID-19 negatively impacted the entire planet. One impact was travel, which affected Walt Disney World attendance. Like so many companies during this time, Disney had very few options and had to make a painful and unavoidable decision if they wanted to continue having a Walt Disney World.

And I wasn't the only one affected. It felt like with each passing day, I would hear from someone I worked with who was in the same boat as me.

What a terrible time, wasn't it? Truly terrible.

As the clouds of that terrible time began to lift, several of my peers received phone calls inviting them back to work for Disney, and others found different opportunities that led them down new, exciting paths.

For me, it brought my career back "full circle." I returned to work as a freelance writer, a job I had before moving to Orlando in 2000 to work for Disney. I did receive a call in the summer of 2021 asking if I was interested in returning to Disney. I respectfully declined. I was extremely flattered, but just like Pocahontas (another two points if you were expecting that reference) I believed that my dream was pointing me down another path.

This was not an easy decision or one I took lightly. I miss being a part of Disney and the people I worked with who did, indeed, become that Disney family through the years.

That fall of 2020, much like the other personal challenges, gave me some of the greatest lessons and moments of wisdom in my entire life.

I learned that everything happens for a reason. You may not know what that reason is as it happens (like when you lose your job and are focused on just how many days you can go without shaving), but it eventually makes itself known.

Though the situation was different, TV and podcast host Conan O'Brien (another two points if you saw *that* reference coming) best summed up the lesson I learned from all these challenges.

In 2010, during a much-publicized moment in late-night talk show history, O'Brien exited as host of *The Tonight Show*, after only seven months, and after a protracted period of negotiations with NBC, as the show's ratings had slipped. Jay Leno would return to *The Tonight Show*.

O'Brien was unhappy and disappointed (as were his fans) with how everything transpired. January 22, 2010, was his last show as host and he addressed his audience with humor, class, and dignity. And, with words that still stay with me:

"All I ask of you is one thing: please don't be cynical. I hate cynicism – it's my least favorite quality and doesn't lead anywhere. Nobody in life gets exactly what they thought they were going to get. But if you work really hard and you're kind, amazing things will happen."[46]

Profound. Life never works out how we envision it and often changes our plans. It's what we do with that new set of plans that matters.

And, during these unexcepted twists and turns, we may even find some Magic Moments.

---

[46] Lynette Rice, "Conan O'Brien's Final monologue: 'Nobody in life gets what they thought they were going to get,'" *Entertainment Weekly*, ew.com, July 30, 2020 (accessed January 27, 2023).

CHAPTER THIRTEEN

"Every Bit of Life Is Lit by Fortuosity"
Magic Moments

"Where Magic Lives." That was a Walt Disney World marketing campaign in 2003. It's wonderful, but just the sound of it could conjure up cynics and scoffers.

Really? A theme park and resort? Where Magic Lives? Rides, restaurants, and characters? Where Magic Lives? Souvenirs, parades, and hotel rooms? Where Magic Lives? Hot, muggy days in the summer and crowded nights during the holidays? Where Magic Lives?

Really?

Yes, really.

Get ready to scoff, laugh, or snark, but I saw magic happen during my twenty years with Disney.

We all know that magic in real life is an ethereal thing. When it is discussed, it's often in situations where fantasy has seemingly invaded our reality, such as a castle in the middle of Central Florida.

Sure, we all realistically know that the magic we know of, particularly with Disney, is usually the stuff found in Disney's movies – Blue Faries, Fairy Godmothers, Beasts who transform into princes and queens who control the snow – but the magic I was lucky enough to be a part of at Disney brought this same sense of wonder.

It grew out of times of serendipity, those rare occasions when the stars align and everything works out.

But, trust me, they really were magic moments.

They were fortuitous moments. There is a line from the song "Fortuosity" from the Disney live-action musical, *The Happiest Millionaire* by Richard and Robert Sherman (score another ten points if you saw that reference coming) that sums up what these magic moments are:

> "Fortuosity, that's me byword.
> Fortuosity, me twinkle in the eye word.
> Sometimes castles fall to the ground,
> But that's where four-leaf clovers are found.
> Fortuosity, lucky chances.
> Fortuitous little happy happenstances.
> I don't worry 'cause everywhere I see,
> that every bit of life is lit by fortuosity." [47]

Through the always brilliant and insightful lyrics of The Sherman Brothers, "Fortuosity" (which is heard as part of the background music every Magic Kingdom day on Main Street, U.S.A.) speaks to what those moments of magic were.

We all have these in our lives or workplaces, where we look to create a moment for a family member, friend, customer, or client, and everything not only falls into place but somewhat exceeds what we had initially envisioned.

When they happen while you are working against the backdrop of Walt Disney World, one can't help but feel that, despite what cynics say, magic is happening.

One of these magic moments that has become indelible involved my time as the Magic Kingdom Merchandise Training Manager, just before we opened the Bibbidi-Bobbidi-Boutique inside Cinderella Castle.

The Bibbidi-Bobbidi-Boutique has become a favorite among Guests, especially those with a young member of their party who has always longed to be a Disney Princess. The concept is what is termed a "transformational experience" for Guests.

In what looks like a hair salon (for lack of a much better term) with a fairy tale "overlay," these young Guests can have their hair styled, glittered, and "tiara-ed" (another word I just coined), along with a dress inspired by their favorite Disney Princess to go along with it.

The Cast Members who provided this experience were called Fairy Godmothers in Training. As their name suggested, they

---

47 Lyrics from "Fortuosity," Disney.fandom.com (accessed April 20, 2023).

were training with none other than the Fairy Godmother herself to help each Guest become a princess. They would guide their young Guest through the entire transformation process, from introduction to the final "reveal," where they turned the Guest around in their chair to see themselves as a Princess for the first time in the mirror.

With the complexities of their roles, from theming to learning the different hairstyles to assisting a young Guest who may be timid, nervous, or scared of the whole experience, the Fairy Godmothers in Training received a lot of, well, training. Their role was all about creating this memorable and, yes, magical experience for all of the Guests and their families who had dreamed of a moment like this since watching the Disney animated fairy tales and fables.

That's where my team came in. This was the second Bibbidi-Bobbidi-Boutique. The first opened at what is now Disney Springs and had been a huge success. A Magic Kingdom location, especially inside Cinderella Castle, was the focus of much anticipation as we readied it.

As the Fairy Godmothers in Training came to the end of their training, we knew that we had to do something special to emphasize the uniqueness of their roles and also create magic for them before they did the same for Guests.

The leadership team had the idea of giving out diplomas to signify "graduation," and we were even able to secure space backstage with a stage to invite each Fairy Godmother in Training to present the certificate.

At the time, David, a member of the Training leadership team, was responsible for Entertainment training. We had partnered together, and his team assisted with a portion of the training for the Fairy Godmothers in Training.

I was telling David about the surprise graduation ceremony we had planned for the Fairy Godmothers in Training. He smiled and said, "I think I know how to make it even more of a surprise."

Earlier I mentioned that, when having one of those "I have an idea" moments, it was important to share it with someone else. Sometimes that can result in a magic moment, which happened here.

On graduation day, the leadership team gathered on the stage, and David served as emcee. The Fairy Godmothers in Training sat in the theater, a combination of nervousness and excitement at being just a few days away from the opening of the second Bibbidi-Bobbidi-Boutique.

As the leadership team was about to begin calling each Fairy Godmother in Training up onto the stage, David let us all know that two special guests would like to help present the diplomas.

And out onto the stage came Cinderella and her Fairy Godmother.

The theater erupted in cheers as if it was the start of a concert, and then the realization of the moment set in, tears began to well up in the eyes of the Fairy Godmothers in Training. Each one was called by name. Cinderella and her Fairy Godmother presented the certificate, gave hugs and congratulations, and picture after picture was taken, capturing the moment forever.

The afternoon of the last day of on-the-job training, and a team gathering together, was transformed into a Magic Moment.

Every day, these Magic Moments happened when you least expected them.

I experienced another one while working at the Walt Disney World shops at Orlando International Airport. One day, one of the Coordinators, Romy, came to me to tell me that a young Guest was in the shop with a letter.

When I went over to talk to the young girl, she told me she had written a letter to Tinker Bell and the other Disney fairies before she flew home. Could she leave the note with us, and could we ensure that Tinker Bell and her friends received it?

She even added that she knew exactly which tree in Fantasyland Tinker Bell lived in and showed me a photo on her mother's phone. Additionally, she had a return envelope, hoping that if Tinker Bell and her friends had a chance, they could write back to her.

Romy and I, of course, took her letter and return envelope and let her know that we would ensure that her correspondence got to Ms. Bell. We waved goodbye to the young Guest and her grateful family, and as they made their way toward TSA, Romy and I turned to each other with the same thought: "What the heck do we do now?"

The only thing that came to mind was to reach out to Magic Kingdom Guest Relations. As luck would have it, there was a leader there I knew, Nathaniel.

He had served as a Walt Disney World Ambassador and loved creating moments like this for Guests. He asked that we drop off the letter, and he would take it from there. Not long after that, we received an e-mail from Nathaniel, letting us know how he followed up, and when Romy and I read the note, our jaws dropped.

Nathaniel had located the tree that the young Guest referenced, took a picture of the letter in the envelope, propped up against it, and left it there for Tinker Bell. He also had another picture of just the tree, so we knew Tinker Bell retrieved the letter.

He also sent us the response from Tinker Bell to the young Guest, which would be accompanied by an autograph in the Tinker Bell flourishes of a signature. All of this had been sent to the Guest in the envelope she had provided.

Romy and I thought about that young girl's (and her parents') reaction when that envelope arrived in their mailbox.

All of this came from a chance encounter, where a young girl stopped into a shop before getting on a plane to go home, giving an envelope to two strangers. Her parents hoped that she would get a response, and the young girl knew that she would.

She believed in magic. As she grew older, she may have recalled that story with her family, potentially realizing there really is magic in this world.

And all that magic happens when others take a chance to do something for a stranger.

And, just like the Fairy Godmothers in Training, these moments of taking a chance would also result in magic for Cast Members.

In the spring of 2015, during my Downtown Disney (now Disney Springs) leader days, I was asked to be part of the selection committee for the Walt Disney Legacy Award. This was an award given to a small group of select Cast Members who are seen as those who carry on Walt's vision to dream, create and inspire.

The Walt Disney Legacy Award is prestigious recognition because the recipients are nominated by their peers.

A group of Cast Members who serve as the selection committee are sequestered like a jury, review the nominations, and make the final decisions. A lofty task is followed by the loftier task of presenting the Walt Disney Legacy Award.

The recipients would each receive not only a beautiful, framed sketch of Walt Disney, with their name embossed on it, but also a special nametag, which was blue and included a pin of Mickey as the Sorcerer from *Fantasia* at the top.

Not something that could be shot out of a t-shirt canon. The presentation needed to be done in a meaningful way.

To add to the challenge, only a select few knew who would receive the recognition, so we had to keep the presentation a surprise.

One of the Walt Disney Legacy Award recipients would be Christina, a Merchandise Manager at Downtown Disney. A person of constant, infectious, upbeat spirit, the "small circle" planning knew the presentation had to be worthy of her.

Whenever possible, we had been attempting to invite family to these presentations. But, so many families lived out of state, as many Cast Members relocated to Orlando to work for Disney.

Christina's family lived in North Carolina, but her leader Jeff said he would call them to let them know that she was receiving the award and, possibly, see if they could FaceTime during the presentation.

A day later, Jeff let me know that he spoke with Christina's parents, who weren't interested in Face Timing...they would *be* at the presentation.

Since the presentation was in the next few days, Christina's parents would be dropping everything and spending an entire day driving from North Carolina to Florida so that they could be there.

The following morning, as we all gathered outside the carousel in the Marketplace section of Downtown Disney, the

Vice President read Christina's name, and she came forward from the crowd in complete shock, laughing, tears in her eyes.

As she was given her new nametag and picture, her parents emerged from the crowd (where they had been strategically hidden).

"WHAAATTT?!?" Christina exclaimed in the middle of her impromptu acceptance speech, as in no way did she expect her parents to be there. As they hugged and everyone applauded, it was an emotional capper to the morning.

I worked with Christina afterward, and she talked of how surreal it was to see her parents, who were supposed to be several states away, at home, on a random weekday morning, step out and smile at her and how it was one of the "top days," she will never forget.

For all of us there that morning, hearing that her parents spent an entire day driving down the east coast to be with her and seeing them there together. Well, it was magic.

Planning like this went into similar moments for Guests. However, for every "aww"-inspiring marriage proposal in front of Cinderella Castle and emotional presentation of the American flag to a military veteran at the evening flag retreat ceremony on Main Street, U.S.A., there are smaller moments that leave their positive impacts on Guests.

Moments like this could occur almost daily when at the International Gateway shop at Epcot. International Gateway is the shop in the back of the World Showcase that allows Guests entrance to several nearby Disney resorts (and now allows access to the Skyliner).

One of the Cast Members who worked in the shop, named Ron, thought up something special one day, on the fly, that became one of the "standards" at International Gateway.

One night, as a young girl watched Ron scan items at the register that she and her family were purchasing, Ron asked if she would like to help him. He brought her behind the counter and let her hold the scanner, showing her where to scan the barcode on each item. Then when she was finished, he asked if she would help put the things in a bag.

As they did this, Dad started taking pictures, capturing the moment.

After the parents paid, Ron told the young girl, "Now, when you go home, you can tell everyone that you worked at Walt Disney World."

From Ron's initiative that evening, inspired to make magic for Guests, came the "Cast Member of the Day."

It grew to include a large, oversized paper nametag with the name "Cast Member" on it (which would be affixed to the young Guest's shirt through the magic of rolled-up Scotch tape) and a certificate they would receive at the "end of their shift," which would last as long as it took to scan the merchandise they were purchasing.

We International Gateway Cast Members adopted "The Cast Member of the Day" as part of our workday. Each day would include a young Guest "working" with us for a few minutes and presented with a certificate.

Applause, certificate, smile, picture.

As we would all go about the rest of our day, none of us realized how these few minutes became part of a family's memories. Then, one morning, while standing outside the shop as Epcot opened for the day, one of the Cast Members stood by the door and waved to a family as they entered the park.

The Cast Member overhead a conversation the family had as they walked by, with the young girl saying, "Hey, Mom, isn't that the shop I worked in the last time we were here a few years ago?"

And suddenly, they realized they were referring to "The Cast Member of the Day." The young girl remembered. Just a few minutes spent with us. Something so simple that it took just a few minutes but was a memory for a family years after.

These stories really do happen during every Walt Disney World day, where Cast Members take extra time and creativity to bring this magic to life for others. A beloved lost baseball cap returns to the Guest with a note that includes a story of the adventure it's been on; a character that a Guest didn't have a chance to meet in the park suddenly signs an autograph that appears in that Guest's resort room; those same rooms might feature elaborately crafted characters created from towels, or find the room decorated for a birthday or an anniversary, maybe just because a Cast Member at the front desk "overheard

Mickey mention something,"; and that same Mouse mentioning something might also get that Guest invited onstage to be part of a show to celebrate a special day, or maybe even serenaded by a server, who leads an entire restaurant in a celebratory chorus of "Happy Birthday."

There are also life moments. In addition to engagements that happen in front of Cinderella Castle, sometimes in the evening, just as fireworks illuminate the sky, a Disney character on a parade float may spot their biggest fan eagerly waiting below, and point to them as they wave.

In their book, *A Portrait of Walt Disney World: 50 Years of the Most Magical Place on Earth*, authors Kevin M. Kern, Tim O'Day, and Steve Vagnini sum up the ethereal feeling Cast Members provide to Guests when they visit:

"The giddy anticipation of arriving through the WELCOME portals begets excited chatter amongst eager travelers; they are primed to disengage and revel in its fun because of the decades-long, hard-earned reputation of the realm they are about to enter. To enjoy this place in the company of loved ones is the ultimate form of wish fulfillment, an opportunity to feel most alive. The awe of discovery, the tonic of laughter, and the joy of togetherness – each complex and almost fleeting emotions – are what govern the hope and happiness provided by this Vacation Kingdom."[48]

Yes, Walt Disney World is the place "Where magic lives."

---

48 Kevin Kern, Tim O'Day, Steve Vagnini, *A Portrait of Walt Disney World: 50 Years of the Most Magical Place on Earth*, (New York, Disney Editions, 2021), p. 302.

CHAPTER FOURTEEN

Keep Moving Forward

When I worked at Epcot, I remember meeting a Guest who spotted my hometown of "Long Island, NY" on my nametag. He was visiting from Queens, NY, which is near Long Island, and during our conversation, he told me that he had just retired from working in the toll booth at one of New York's bridges.

It was his first Walt Disney World visit, and he told me he came through the park's toll plaza when driving into Epcot's parking lot this morning.

"I didn't know that there were toll booths *here*," he laughed. "I should have moved down here years ago and worked *here*!"

The exchange made me realize that so many people not only dream of visiting Walt Disney World but working there, as well.

I feel very fortunate to have made that dream come true for myself.

Being a Walt Disney World Cast Member is a unique experience, particularly for a Disney fan. It's especially gratifying when working with fellow Disney fans, as I did. That's one of the differences about working for Disney. There's a shared passion, not just for *what* you do for work but also for *where* you work.

People from everywhere seek out a Walt Disney World job for different reasons, but for most there is one common denominator: Disney.

From the "grown-up kids" (like this author) who have held tightly to Disney their whole life to those who have an interest in Disney, to those who want to discover more, that connection to what Disney means to so many, is part of every Cast Member's DNA.

My good friend, Kyle (who has provided the lasting memory of "Tradsgiving" discussed earlier), perfectly summed up the feeling of being a Cast Member when he told the *Disney Parks Blog*: "You can't necessarily make a career out of the things you love, but I just happened to fall in love with a company that offers experiences and joy to people around the world."[49]

Sure, the company, like all companies, has changed throughout the years. It has transitioned from a small garage, where Walt and Roy Disney started in 1923, to theme parks around the world, television networks, cruise ships, streaming services, and the realms of Muppets, Pixar, Marvel, Lucasfilm, and 20th Century Studios, which exist alongside Disney characters and theme parks today.

With all this change, working at Disney has its ups and downs, as is the case with most companies. Heck, there are ups and downs in life.

Through it all, I truly loved working for Disney, and even through the "lowest of low" times, I wouldn't have traded the experience for anything. Those "highs" made it all worth it.

This is why I wanted to share the stories in this book, not just to accentuate my story at Disney but the stories of so many others who worked so hard to selflessly create daily experiences for others.

If you've made it this far, I hope my stories will only increase your Walt Disney World appreciation, and your next trip will be filled with wonder at how all that wonder is created.

Successful and not-so-successful moments came out of each of these. The lessons are shared in the hopes that they can be enjoyed and passed along. Even if there wasn't a familiar moment from these lessons, there might be a time in the future when you, dear reader, can recall that lesson, and it will aid in a solution or assist with making sense of the nonsense, in any area of your life.

I believe in sharing what we've learned in life and passing it on to others to possibly find a guidepost.

---

49 Kami Ellender, "Disney Cast Member Shares Photography Tips From National Geographic Expedition," *Disney Parks Blog*, disneyparks.disney.go.com, May 24, 2023 (accessed May 26, 2023).

These experiences and lessons were generated by memories I hold dear. I had opportunities at Disney that I never tire of sharing. Walt Disney was a storyteller at heart, and while Walt is no longer with us, the gift he has left for Cast Members is to continue the story he started for The Disney Company.

For millions, Disney remains the same light of hope as the lamp that illuminates the Disneyland firehouse. One of Walt's most famous quotes (used beautifully in the studio's 2007 animated film *Meet the Robinsons*) is:

"Around here, however, we don't look backwards for very long. We keep moving forward, opening up new doors and doing new things..."[50]

Walt, the storyteller, has also left a gift for non-Cast Members: we can all tell our own story, craft it as we want, and share it with others. Memories help us do this, and memories are meant to be shared. "Keep moving forward" and sharing those memories of your own.

While I no longer work for Disney and have returned to a career as a freelance writer, I still feel very close to Disney, and not just in a geographical sense, as I live in Central Florida. I will forever be a part of it. You may leave the company physically, but it always stays in your heart. There's not a day that I don't think of someone or something from my twenty years there. My experiences inform me daily and inspire my thoughts (and this book!).

It's been quite the journey from my Walt Disney World trip in 1987, when my dad excitedly proclaimed, "We're here!" Two decades took me from nights on Main Street, U.S.A., to days in Dinoland, U.S.A., and from a World Showcase at Epcot to a Galaxy's Edge at Disney's Hollywood Studios.

When I taught Traditions class, we would conclude each session with an inspirational video of families enjoying all that Walt Disney World had to offer. The music accompanying this was a beautiful ballad, "Share a Dream Come True." The lyrics strike a chord:

---

50 Jerry Beck, "Keep Moving Forward," *Cartoon Brew*, cartoonbrew.com, March 24, 2007 (accessed May 25, 2023).

"We share a magic day.
We share enchanted nights.
It's a never-ending story.
That together, we all write.
It's been a part of me.
It's been a part of you.
A part of growing up together,
sharing a dream come true."[51]

And each day's "dreams come true" that I experienced as a Cast Member at Walt Disney World brought with them stories, lessons, and memories, which were simply magic... Magic Moments.

---

51 Lyrics to "Share a Dream Come True," Disboards.com (accessed June 23, 2023).

Bibliography

Books

Cockerell, Dan, *How's the Culture in Your Kingdom?: Lessons from a Disney Leadership Journey*, New York: Morgan James Publishing, 2021.

Cockerell, Lee, *Creating Magic: 10 Common Sense Strategies from a Life at Disney*, New York: Doubleday, 2008.

Finch, Christopher, *The Art of Walt Disney: From Mickey Mouse to The Magic Kingdoms*, New York: Harry N. Abrams, Inc. Publishers.

Iger, Robert, *The Ride of a Lifetime*, New York: Random House, 2019.

Kern, Kevin, Tim O'Day, Steve Vagnini, *A Portrait of Walt Disney World: 50 Years of the Most Magical Place on Earth*, New York: Disney Editions, 2021.

Kurtti, Jeff, *Since the World Began: Walt Disney World The First 25 Years*, New York: Hyperion, 1996.

Nabbe, Tom, *From Disneyland's Tom Sawyer to Disney Legend: The Adventures of Tom Nabbe*, Orlando: Theme Park Press, 2015.

Smith, Dave, *Disney A to Z: The Disney Encyclopedia*, New York: Disney Editions, 2006.

Sullivan, William "Sully," *From Jungle Cruise Skipper to Disney Legend: 40 Years of Magical Memories at Disney*, Orlando: Theme Park Press, 2015.

Thomas, Bob, *Walt Disney: An American Original*, New York: Hyperion, 1994.

Articles

Amadeo, Kimberly, "The Stock Market Crash of 2008," thebalancemoney.com, May 25, 2022 (accessed on January 18, 2023).

Beck, Jerry, "Disney 1970s Summer Film Festivals," *Cartoon Brew*, cartoonbrew.com, October 1, 2008, (accessed May 12, 2023).

---, "Keep Moving Forward," *Cartoon Brew*, cartoonbrew.com, March 24, 2007 (accessed May 25, 2023).

Burris, Eric, "Charley Made Landfall 18 Years Ago in Florida," wesh.com, August 13, 2022 (accessed June 21, 2023).

Ellender, Kami, "Disney Cast Member Shares Photography Tips From National Geographic Expedition," *Disney Parks Blog*, disneyparks.disney.go.com, May 24, 2023 (accessed May 26, 2023).

Figueroa, Jessica, "PHOTO: Lamp Remains Lit in Walt Disney's Apartment at Disneyland During Extended Park Closure," wdwnt.com, April 1, 2020 (accessed on January 10, 2023).

Jo, Sophie, "A Second Home: Walt Disney's Fire Station Apartment," waltdisney.org, June 20, 2020 (accessed on January 10, 2023).

Korkis, Jim, "WDW Chronicles: When Hurricane Floyd Came to Town," Allears.net, September 25, 2022 (accessed November 30, 2022).

Kunerth, Jeff, "Jess Rubio: Disney Caricaturist Turned Talent Into A Franchise," *The Orlando Sentinel*, October 24, 2010, orlandosentinel.com (accessed February 14, 2023).

Pederson, Joe Mario "The Year 3 Hurricane Paths Crossed One Spot in Central Florida," Tampabay.com, Sept. 24, 2019 (accessed November 22, 2022).

---, "'Nightmare Scenario': 15 Years Since Florida Was Beaten, Bruised By 4 Hurricanes In 6 Weeks," orlandosentinel.com, August 13, 2019 (Accessed December 13, 2019).

Rice, Lynette, "Conan O'Brien's Final monologue: 'Nobody in life gets what they thought they were going to get," *Entertainment Weekly*, ew.com, July 30, 2020 (accessed January 27, 2023).

Web Sites

Brainyquote.com
D23.com
Disboards.com
Disney.fandom.com
Genius.com
IMDb.com
Laughbreak.com
Merriam-webster.com
Musixmatch.com
Quotes.net
Speakola.com
Urbandictionary.com
Wikipedia.com
Youtube.com

Acknowledgments

It would take more than twenty years to thank all the people who supported and inspired me during my twenty years working at Walt Disney World and those who helped in making this book a reality.

In addition to my mom, Kay Lyons, and my dad and stepmom, Bill and Sandy Lyons, to whom this book is dedicated, I am, as I am every day, grateful to my wife, Michelle, who, as I've said, always has more faith in me than I have in myself.

My family: Aunts, Uncles, Grandparents, Cousins, and Stepbrothers, who have always loved and supported *my* love of Disney. Thank you for such special memories of growing up in Long Island. We may no longer live close by, but we are all still close in heart.

I am incredibly thankful to Bob McLain and Theme Park Press for being such a kind, patient, and supportive publisher and for allowing my writing to have a home.

Friends and family who have taken the time to read the book in its various stages and provide insight, including author, friend, Disney, animation and music historian Greg Ehrbar who provided invaluable insight, as always; Ali Peters, who, once again, was the cheerleader I needed; my cousin Ken Kehoe, a fellow Disney fan (and English teacher) helped shepherd the book; writer and fellow Disney fan James Warda provided invaluable advice; Angie Robinson, whose talents as a leadership and life coach, coupled with her passion for Disney, equipped me with great perspective; and Maryann DeShannon, a valued friend and mentor, who brought her leadership and Disney experiences to her input.

She is one of many I was fortunate enough to work with and be inspired by during my two decades with Disney. The impact of these individuals is the cornerstone of this book.

They include Mike Myers, Mike Cramer, Dru Long, Tammy Haven-Long, Brian Gage, Cathy Wilson, Dan Cockerell, Jim Hogan, Penny Slocum, Randy Gonzalez, Scott Bleakney, Steve Taylor, Susan Shadrick, Mickey Metz, Mike Reardon, Neil A. Johnson, Lenny Lamothe, Rutledge Boykin, Suzette Noble, Lisa Ackley, Beverly Martin, David Cohen, Nathaniel Palma, Jeff Starks, Christina Griffin, Dana Rigney, Lonnie Hicks, Stacey Sievers Romano, Steven Miller, Janet Kelley, Robert Kelley, Mary Roche, Romy Varela, Rebecca Godsil, Anthony Seaton, David Beisel, Angie Klote, Lorraine Oakley, and Martin McCarthy.

Fellow Cast Members who have become family: Rene and Robert Villa, Scott Hopkins, Kyle Raser, Brandon Raser Hackett, Nate Rasmussen, Kelly Moore, Christopher White, and the entire White family, Toni, Luci, Cameron, and Annie.

Once again, I am so grateful for my best friends Andy DiGenova and Hunter Fagan for inviting me to be a part of the podcast "Dis-Order: Every Disney Film," as well as all the "Dis-Order" listeners and the entire "Real Fans 4 Real Movies" podcast network.

To every Cast Member I was fortunate enough to work with and every Guest I was fortunate enough to encounter during my two decades working at Walt Disney World - thank you for the laughs, the stories, and the memories that continue to shape my every day.

And, to the memory of two individuals who have each had an incredibly positive impact on my life:

Jim Korkis, whose gifts as a historian, speaker, teacher, researcher, and writer were like a superpower, but whose greatest strength was his power of friendship. His kindness and guidance through the years led me down paths where I would continually learn more about the world and myself.

And Walt Disney, whose imagination and legacy, as it does for so many others, still serves as "a source of joy and inspiration!"

Thank you, one and all!

About the Author

Michael Lyons is a freelance writer specializing in film, television, and pop culture. He has contributed over 500 articles to such publications as *Cinefantastique, Disney Magazine, ReMIND*, the websites animationworldnetwork.com and fandom.com, and is a writer for the Web Stories division of Static Media.

He is the author of the book, *Drawn to Greatness: Disney's Animation Renaissance*, (also published by Theme Park Press) which chronicles the unprecedent growth in Disney animation during the 1990s.

Michael has also interviewed many artists, directors, and producers in the entertainment industry. These interviews are featured in several volumes of the book series *Walt's People: Talking Disney With the Artists Who Knew Him*.

From 2000-2020, Michael continued to write while working full-time at the Walt Disney World Resort in Orlando, Florida. Here, he held several leadership positions, both in the operation and with Disney's training organization. Michael worked at all four of Walt Disney World's theme parks, Disney's retail and dining center, Disney Springs, as well as off-site company locations at Orlando International Airport.

Additionally, Michael served as a leader with many major company initiatives, such as those focused on guest service and the introduction of new technology. He was also part of the teams that re-imagined Disney's flagship retail location, The World of Disney, and the opening of Star Wars: Galaxy's Edge.

Michael is also a recipient of the Walt Disney Legacy Award.

In 2020, Michael focused full-time on his writing. Michael writes and edits his blog, "Screen Saver: A Retro Review of TV Shows and Movies of Yesteryear," which can be found at screensaverblog.blogspot.com. Additionally, he contributes a weekly column to the website "Cartoon Research "(cartoonresearch.

com) and co-hosts the podcasts "Dis-Order: Every Disney Film," and "From Pencils to Pixels: The Animation Celebration Podcast" (both available at rf4rm.com).

Michael lives with his wife, Michelle, in Winter Garden, Florida. You can visit Michael's website at:

www.wordsfromlyons.com

Made in the USA
Columbia, SC
18 May 2024

35862836R00108